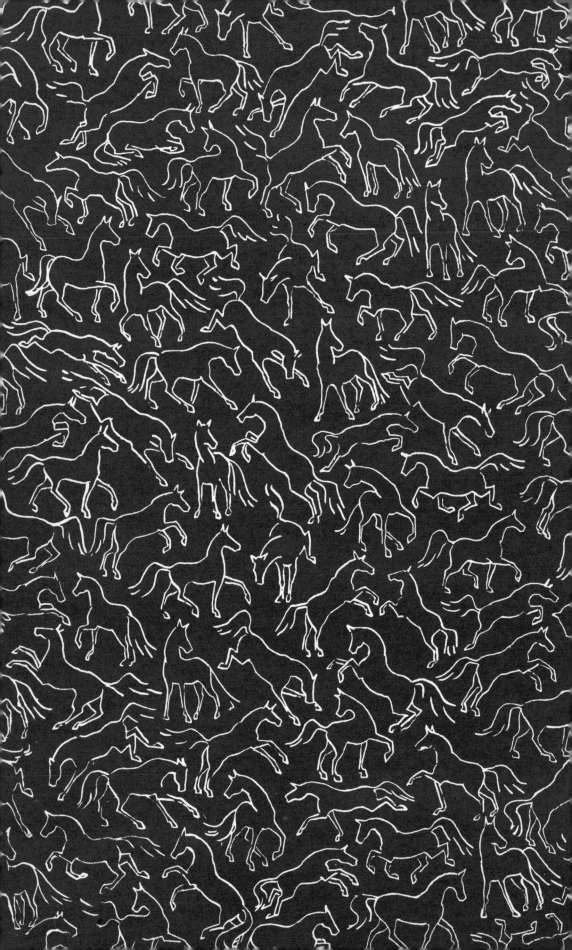

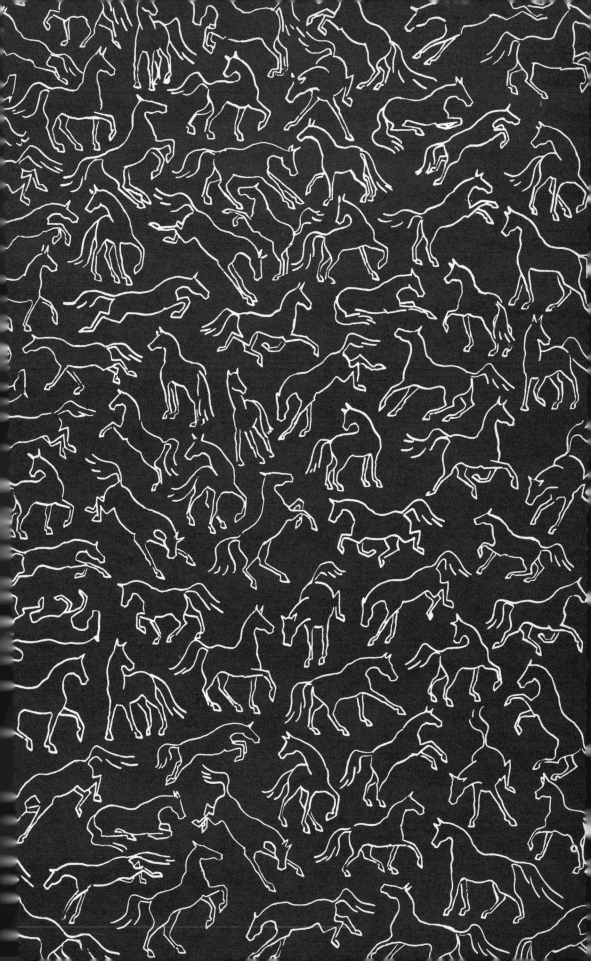

Horsemanship for Beginners

RIDING, JUMPING, AND SCHOOLING

PHOTOGRAPHS BY

Michael J. Phillips

ALFRED A. KNOPF : NEW YORK

Horsemanship
FOR BEGINNERS
RIDING, JUMPING, and SCHOOLING

Jean Slaughter

To those young riders who will, one day,

ride as members of the Olympic

Team

THIS IS A BORZOI BOOK,
PUBLISHED BY ALFRED A. KNOPF, INC.

798
51a
c. 1
5-26-71

Eighth Impression

L. C. catalogue number: 52–6390

Foreword

Rider, exhibitor, teacher and keen observer of horsemanship, Miss Slaughter has created a book which will undoubtedly be a strong incentive to the novice. The principles of horsemanship are clearly stated in lively style. The book teaches not only good horsemanship, but how to derive full benefit from the sport. Obviously, Miss Slaughter has enjoyed writing the book as much as she enjoys riding. It should prove of great value in encouraging the talent needed for the future to complete teams for international equestrian events.

COLONEL JOHN W. WOFFORD
Team Captain,
U.S. Equestrian Team.

Acknowledgment

I wish to express my deepest appreciation to all those who, in so many ways, helped in the preparation of this book.

—To Elaine Phillips, for her unfailing interest and endless patience; and to Michael J. Phillips, for the countless hours spent in illustrating and designing this book;

—To the Board of Stewards and the members of the Ox Ridge Hunt Club, Darien, Connecticut, where most of these pictures were taken;

—To the children who lent their horses, and rode for so many hours before the camera: Chilla Blair, Nini De Jurenev, Linda FitzRandolph, Sandy Glynn, Victor Hugo-Vidal, Jr., Barbara, Julie, and Rick Kellam, Fred Kelly, Nancy and Susan Lounsbury, Glenna Lee Maduro, George Morris, Ronnie Mutch, Pamela Phillips, Betsy Quayle, Patricia Slaughter, and Lyn Westerlund.

—And to Miss Felicia Townsend and Otto Heuckeroth, of Ox Ridge, for their encouragement and interest.

I also wish to thank Freudy Photos, Inc., of New York, for the use of the photographs on pages 5 and 111.

Contents

Is Good Horsemanship Important?

"Jimmy never took a lesson in his life and he can stay on any horse."

"Ann doesn't care about learning good horsemanship. She just wants to ride."

How often you hear these words said and how funny they are when you really think about them!

Just because you can ride in a car doesn't mean you can drive it. Just because Ann and Jimmy can stay on a horse and make him "go" doesn't mean they are riders.

Horsemanship is more than looking well on a horse, more than arranging your legs and hands in a proper position. A rider who wants to learn good horsemanship knows that his horse is an intelligent, friendly animal, willing to learn and fun to ride, but with a mind of his own. To such a rider, merely getting on his horse's back and making him go is not enough. He wants to know how to teach his horse to go well, cheerfully but obediently, so both he and his horse will get the most pleasure from the hours they spend together.

With a foundation of good horsemanship you can go on into wider fields with confidence in yourself and your horse, learning through experience that the magic of a horseman's hands is no more than patience and thought and common sense.

Hunting, showing, riding through bridle paths alone or with a friend, the security and confidence of horsemanship knowledge can increase your riding pleasure a hundred times over.

Enjoy every moment of your learning, for the day will *never* come when you can say, "Now I know everything." There will always be something new, one more challenge, one more question to be answered.

All this pleasure and knowledge is there for you if you care enough. It is up to you.

The Forward Seat

There have always been arguments, and I suppose there always will be, as to which is the best style of riding. There are those who say the Westerners have the answer; for those who must spend long hours in the saddle as they work, this style certainly serves its purpose.

Another type of riding is the saddle seat, used on the gleaming, high-stepping Saddle Horses. These are primarily show horses and the rider must adapt his horsemanship to "lift" their action and exhibit their brilliance and proud way of going.

For general riding, however, most people prefer to ride the hunter-type of horse. To call this style "Eastern" is absolute nonsense, as there are hunters and jumpers in all parts of the country.

A great number of years have been spent in the study of horsemanship, and the result has been the development of the forward, or balanced seat, used in riding hunters and jumpers. This may sound technical and confusing, but it is really very simple.

The forward seat allows full freedom to the horse's natural motions and balance while the rider is in the position to aid, guide, and control him.

There is nothing difficult or startling about this style of riding, and if you've ridden at all you are probably saying, "Why, that's the way I've always ridden; there's nothing new about that!"

You are quite right. More and more riders are learning the advantages of the forward seat and are being taught this way, not only all over this country, but throughout the world.

The forward seat is, then, the style of riding described throughout the following chapters.

Starting Your Ride

There is no substitute for personal supervision when you first start learning to ride. For this reason it is always a good idea to take at least eight or ten lessons from a good riding instructor. The instructor will correct you as you first learn to mount and dismount, and teach you how to hold your reins, how to bridle and saddle your horse, and all the first important steps toward becoming a good rider.

Once you have had these lessons, you will be ready to go on.

Here you are, about to start your ride. Your horse is waiting and you want to be up and off right away. Perhaps he is kept at a stable, or perhaps you take care of him yourself; either way, he is saddled and bridled and ready to go.

Wait a moment before you mount.

Jumping onto your horse and going right off for a ride is a very careless and thoughtless thing to do. Suppose you were sent out for a walk every day, even though there was a stone in your shoe? You would very soon dislike anything to do with walking, of course; yet too many riders do this very thing to their horses.

If the saddle is pinching your horse's shoulders or if the bit is rubbing his tender mouth, he will soon begin to dislike being ridden, as he is hurt whenever he does as you ask. This not only makes your horse uncomfortable and cross, it spoils your own fun as well; a horse annoyed by a carelessly twisted girth will not be much of a pleasure to ride!

Always look your horse over before you get on him. Even though you may have tacked him up yourself, a quick check should be made.

(Bridles, saddles, and martingales are called "tack"; when you

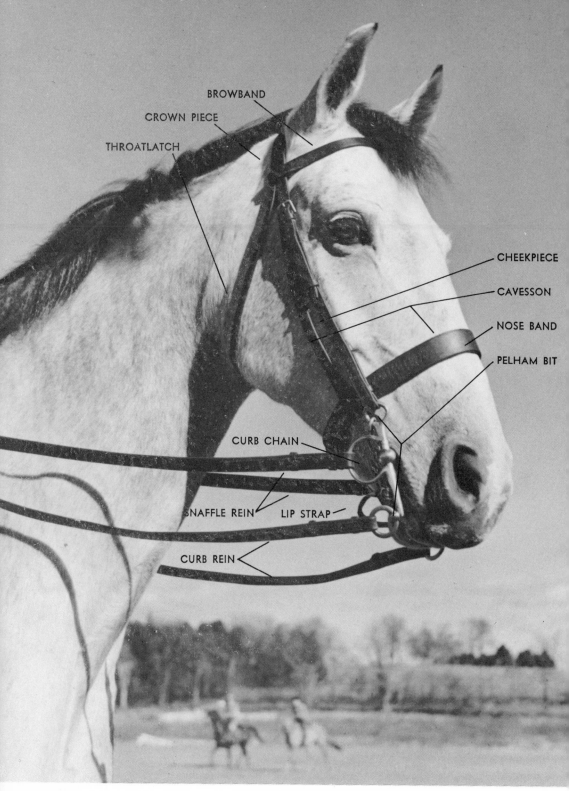

BROWBAND

CROWN PIECE

THROATLATCH

CHEEKPIECE

CAVESSON

NOSE BAND

PELHAM BIT

CURB CHAIN

SNAFFLE REIN

LIP STRAP

CURB REIN

PARTS OF THE BRIDLE

put the saddle and bridle on your horse, you are said to "tack him up.")

The bridle leather should be soft and in good condition. Stiff, dry leather can cut and rub like sandpaper; if your bridle is like this, give it a good going-over with neatsfoot oil and saddle soap.

The **crown piece** of the bridle should lie flat and smooth behind your horse's ears.

The **browband** should be long enough to allow the bridle to lie flat without being so long that it droops on your horse's forehead. Make sure that your horse can move his ears freely without having them pinched by a browband that is too high.

The **throatlatch** should be adjusted so that there is room for your fist between it and your horse's cheek. The throatlatch should never be buckled snugly, as it would then cut into your horse's windpipe when he bent his head.

The **cheekpieces** should be of equal length and adjusted so the bit hangs evenly.

Cavesson is the correct name for the combination of the nose band and the straps that hold it in place. The nose band should be just loose enough to allow two fingers' width between it and your horse's jaw. It should be placed about two inches below the bony ridge of the cheekbone. If it is lower than this it may catch on the bit or rub the tender skin of the muzzle.

The reins, if they fasten to the bit with ordinary buckles, should have these buckles showing on the outside where you can see them. Stud fasteners are neater and more attractive, as they are on the inside of the reins and do not show, but both types serve the same purpose.

If you have two reins, such as on a pelham or double bridle, the slightly broader rein is the snaffle rein and should be on top. The narrower rein is the curb rein and should be below the snaffle.

Now see that all the bridle straps are neatly tucked into their keepers, those small leather loops near the buckles. Flapping straps on a bridle are sloppy, and are the sign of a careless rider.

Make sure that the curb chain, if you have one, lies flat and is properly adjusted.

The position of the bit is very important. Each type of bit must be adjusted differently. In the following chapter this is explained in detail. Read that chapter very carefully, as so many of your signals to your horse are sent through the reins to the bit and an uncomfortable or badly adjusted bit can cause terrible pain.

Now that you have the bridle fitted properly, let's have a look at the saddle.

The best way to put a saddle on is to place it a little too far forward on your horse's back, then slide it into place. This will make the hair lie smoothly.

The girth and under side of the saddle should be clean and soft; get to work with saddle soap if they are not! A folded leather girth should have the folded edge facing toward your horse's elbows.

You should be able to slip all the fingers of one hand under the pommel, or front, of your saddle. This test should be made while you are sitting in the saddle, as your weight will push it down. If you cannot slip your fingers under it easily, you know that the

ALWAYS CHECK TIGHTNESS OF
THE GIRTH BEFORE YOU MOUNT

saddle is coming down too low, pinching the horse's shoulders.

Any good saddle maker can pad your saddle so it will not come down like this. Until this can be done, make your horse comfortable by folding a cloth and placing it over his withers, under the pommel.

Don't be lazy and get into the habit of using this cloth every day, or of using one of those big, bulky saddle pads. Have your saddle fitted to your horse; he will be far more comfortable and it will save you a lot of fuss and bother.

Test the girth. You should just be able to slip your fingers under it and feel it give a little. Check the girth again after you have been riding a few minutes; it may need taking up another hole.

If you make this quick check every day, whether you ride your own horse or one belonging to someone else, it will soon become so automatic that you will be able to spot a twisted curb chain or a loose girth in a moment. This will save you from an unpleasant ride or even from an accident that could easily have been avoided.

GIRTH IS EASILY TIGHTENED
WITHOUT RIDER DISMOUNTING

Bits and Martingales

If you look inside your horse's mouth you will find teeth in the front of his mouth and others farther back. In between these separate rows of teeth is a space where there are no teeth at all. These are the "bars" of your horse's mouth where the bit rests on the lower jaw.

It is very important to know and remember that your horse wears his teeth down unevenly when he eats, leaving sharp edges after a time, on his back teeth especially, where you can't see them. If nothing is done about this, the sharp edges cut the inside of his mouth. A horse with a sore mouth and jagged teeth cannot eat properly and will get thin, no matter how well you feed him. Often a sore-mouthed horse will fret and fuss with his bit, tossing his head in quick jerks; you may have trouble when you bridle him.

For your own sake as well as your horse's, have his teeth checked by a veterinarian once a year. He will "float" your horse's teeth, removing the sharp edges and smoothing them down. You will save yourself a great deal of trouble and your horse a lot of pain if you see that this is done once every twelve months.

The bit you put in your horse's mouth is an aid to control him. It is not a brake! The bit, through your hands and reins, signals your commands to your horse and helps to balance him as well as to turn and stop.

THE CURB BRIDLE

The curb is an extremely severe bit. When the reins are pulled the shanks move back, catching the horse's lower jaw between the bar and curb chain. The curb chain must lie flat and smooth and be adjusted so that it allows two fingers' width between it and the horse's lower jaw. A lip strap is always used with a curb chain; it runs through the extra link in the center of the chain and fastens to the bit shanks, buckling on the left side. It prevents the shanks from turning too far forward.

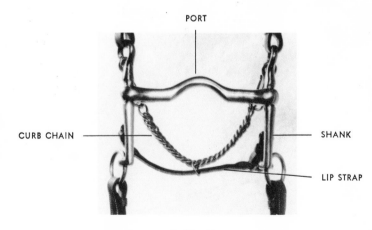

CURB BIT

THE SNAFFLE BRIDLE

The snaffle is a mild bit; the rings are big and heavy so they cannot be pulled into the horse's mouth. This is a jointed egg-butt snaffle; the egg-butt is the round, smooth joining of the mouthpiece and rings to prevent the bit from pinching the corners of the mouth.

Properly adjusted, the snaffle fits snugly at the corners of the mouth, even wrinkling the lips just a little. A single broad rein is used with this bit and is usually laced or braided to give the rider a better grip.

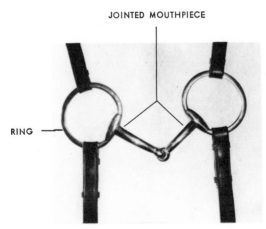

JOINTED MOUTHPIECE

RING

SNAFFLE BIT

THE PELHAM BRIDLE

The pelham is a combination of the snaffle and the curb, in a single bit. The top rein is the snaffle, the lower rein the curb. A curb chain and lip strap are always used with a pelham and adjusted as they would be when used with a curb.

When properly fitted the pelham fits snugly at the corners of the horse's mouth without wrinkling the lips. It should be just wide enough to avoid pinching; a pelham too wide slips back and forth as you pull on the reins.

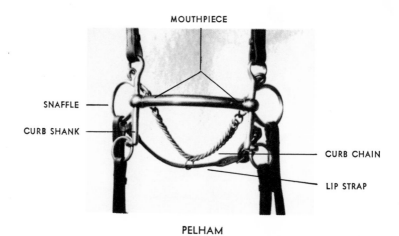

MOUTHPIECE

SNAFFLE

CURB SHANK

CURB CHAIN

LIP STRAP

PELHAM

THE DOUBLE BRIDLE

The double, or full bridle consists of both the snaffle and the curb. The "bridoon" is a special little snaffle-type bit with small rings. It is fitted snugly at the corners of the horse's mouth, just like the ordinary snaffle.

The second bit is the curb and it is adjusted so it hangs evenly in the horse's mouth just below the bridoon. A curb chain and lip strap are always used and adjusted to allow two fingers' width between the chain and lower jaw.

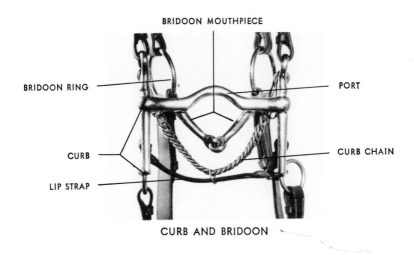

CURB AND BRIDOON

Each horse is an individual and no one definite rule can decide which bit is the best for your horse. The curb, however, should never be used alone. It is far too severe and, because of its action, it is possible to stop a horse with it, but impossible to steady or slow him gently and smoothly. Since quiet steadying of your horse is so terribly important in all your riding, the curb alone must never be used.

There are many other reasons why the curb should never be used alone; they are all based on the fact that a horse ridden in a curb will carry his head at an unnatural angle because he is uncomfortable, afraid of the bit, and trying to escape its action. No horse can jump well in a curb as he cannot carry his head where it belongs to see the fence and judge it properly, or approach it correctly balanced and steadied.

These things do not happen when the curb is used as it is intended to be; with a double bridle or as part of a pelham.

The double bridle puts a great deal of metal into a horse's mouth and the proper use of the two bits is so delicate that only an experienced rider with excellent hands should ever use one. It is a complicated bridle to put on and must always be carefully adjusted; because of these reasons, young riders are better off not using a double bridle until they have had much more experience.

The snaffle is a very mild bit and there are few horses with mouths soft enough to respond to a snaffle the way they should. Your horse may stop and turn in a snaffle, but there is more to riding than just that; and you are apt to find that what you can have your horse do in a snaffle can be done far more smoothly and with far better results in a pelham.

Too often a horse is ridden in a snaffle for one of two very silly reasons; either the rider likes the single rein, or the owner thinks he is being kind by using such a mild bit, though he has to sit back and pull quite hard to stop or turn. How much kinder and more sensible it would be to use a little stronger bit and be able to stop or turn at just a touch of the rein!

Never use a bridoon in place of an ordinary big-ringed snaffle. The little bridoon with its small rings is made to be used only in combination with the curb in a double bridle. If it is used alone it pinches the horse's lips and the little rings can easily be pulled all the way into his mouth. Remember that your horse's mouth is extremely sensitive and such carelessness can cause severe pain.

For a young rider's horse the pelham is often the most useful type of bit.

Pelhams range in severity from the long-shanked bit with a port (the port is the hump in the center of the mouthpiece, and the longer the shank and higher the port, the more severe the bit is), to the short-shanked pelham without a port that is little more severe than the snaffle. A great many horses will go very happily and comfortably in a plain pelham without a port and with a medium shank.

A pelham does have double reins, and for some reason the idea of riding with two reins seems quite impossible to some young riders. "There's too much to hold," they say, and off they go using a curb bit and making their horse miserable, or using a snaffle and making themselves miserable because they can't control their horses properly.

What nonsense this is! You're going to have to learn how to hold double reins eventually, if you ever want to call yourself a rider, and you certainly can't learn any younger. If your hands are small, then get very narrow reins—and in a few days you will wonder why you were so silly about it in the first place!

No matter which bit you decide to use on your horse, be sure it is made of stainless steel. Cheap bits rust and get sharp edges, or break, and putting a rusty or chipped bit in your horse's mouth is a very cruel thing to do. Bits of good quality will last for years and will repay you a hundred times over.

Keep your bit spotlessly clean. Leaf and grass stains are hard to get off, but it serves you right—you shouldn't allow your horse to grab mouthfuls when he is being ridden.

Keep your bridle and reins soft and in good condition with plenty of saddle soap, and a touch of neatsfoot oil if they are dry. Stiff reins are uncomfortable to hold; supple reins are a great help toward good hands.

THE STANDING MARTINGALE IS
FASTENED TO THE NOSE BAND

Someone else's old bit is not the bit for your horse. He is to carry you for many, many hours; the least you can do is make sure he is comfortable with a bit that fits *his* mouth, not the mouth of some other horse.

MARTINGALES

The standing martingale is a long strap which fastens to the girth, runs between the horse's forelegs, and fastens to his nose band. It is kept in place by a narrow strap, called the neck strap, around the horse's neck. This strap always buckles on the left.

A rubber loop, called a "stopper," is used to keep the martingale from sliding through the neck strap.

This martingale prevents your horse from throwing his head too high. If he is extremely fussy when the flies are biting and throws his head up suddenly, a standing martingale will keep you from being hit in the face.

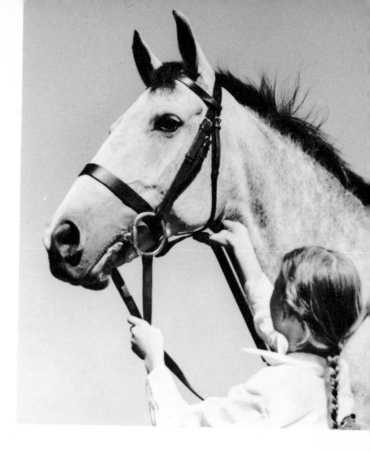

Some horses carry their heads very high to escape the action of the bit; a standing martingale prevents this.

It helps to steady an excitable horse, especially a young one.

Don't use a martingale unless you must; a horse becomes so used to wearing a martingale that he will toss his head when it is taken off, even though he may not have had this annoying habit before.

The martingale's length is adjusted by a buckle at the loop through which the girth is run; this buckle must always be turned away from your horse's chest.

The proper length for a standing martingale is illustrated in the photograph. When your horse's head is held in its natural position, the strap should be just long enough to run from the nose band to the throat latch and down to the girth. It should be tested for proper length as this girl is doing.

If you jump, it should be a hole or two longer than this. **Never jump with a short martingale on your horse.** A horse uses his head

RUNNING MARTINGALE RINGS SHOULD BE LEVEL WITH WITHERS WHEN DRAWN TIGHT

RUNNING MARTINGALE IS USED ON THE SNAFFLE OF PELHAM OR DOUBLE BRIDLE

and neck to balance himself over a fence; if you strap his head down he cannot do this, and he will fall.

The running martingale divides into two short straps, with rings through which the snaffle reins are run. That is the way it is used in this country. In England and Ireland the running martingale is often used on the curb rein.

The running martingale often becomes tangled in awkward places, such as around a post when you open a gate; and if a horse snaps at a fly on his chest, this martingale sometimes catches on his lower jaw, with very unpleasant results.

The correct adjustment of a running martingale is shown here for the benefit of those of you who see others using one and think, because of this, you must use one too.

The Irish martingale is no more than a short strap, about four inches long, with a ring at each end through which the reins are run. This martingale is often seen on steeplechasers, or horses raced over jumps, for when a horse makes a mistake over a fence he recovers his balance with a quick motion of his head which often flips one rein over to the wrong side. The Irish martingale keeps the reins together and prevents this from happening.

The Irish martingale is useful on a horse that tosses one rein over his head either when shaking off a fly, or by giving a quick twist of his head when he bucks.

THE IRISH MARTINGALE IS JUST A SHORT LEATHER STRAP WITH A METAL RING AT EACH END

Kindness and Discipline

Your horse is not a machine and riding is more than just "pressing the right button" to make him go. Riding would be much easier if this were so, but not nearly as much fun.

Each horse is an individual and your horse probably has a special way about him that makes you feel very fond of him; perhaps it is the way he turns his head and pricks his ears when he hears you coming, or perhaps he has an unusually sweet manner when he begs for an apple or a carrot.

It is almost too easy to become too fond of a horse—getting to the point where, in the owner's mind, the horse can do no wrong.

When the owner begins to feel like this, either one of two things will happen. The horse may become the master; or the owner may suddenly wake up and change his ways for the better.

I knew a family who bought a nice horse for their son. They had a big pasture and a lovely stable, and they believed the story books and thought their horse was story-book perfect.

The horse was delighted with all the attention he got. He was fed whenever he was hungry, patted and fussed over, and not asked to do much work. When he was ridden, he soon discovered that if he stopped dead and put his ears back, his owners thought he was tired and would stop riding at once.

The horse soon refused to move a step with a rider on his back. After a few weeks of this his owners began to realize that they were not having as much fun as they expected to have with their new horse.

A month later this horse was advertised for sale, but when people saw what the horse was like they wouldn't buy him. He was finally given away to a riding stable where a lot of work and not much feed taught him some manners.

How much happier and better off this horse would have been, spending his life in his first home, loved and well-cared for, if only his owners had mixed their kindness with a little common sense!

On the other hand, there are some young riders who treat their horses as the cowboys do in the Western movies. The only gait they know is the gallop; they dash down rocky paths, they stop their horses with terrible yanks on severe bits, and always force their horses into a wild gallop from a stand-still. If the horse makes a mistake or does anything wrong, he is immediately spurred or hit with a whip. Most of these horses are thin and nervous because of the strain of hard, inconsiderate riding; you often can see blood on their mouths, and their eyes always look frightened.

One of the most difficult things a young rider must learn is the sensible treatment of his horse. Certainly no rider who treats his horse badly should ever be allowed to own a horse; but young riders must realize that overkindness can be just as cruel in the long run.

Your horse is a big, powerful animal. He was born, raised, and trained to do as he is told. If you allow him to tell *you* what to do, you are asking for trouble—and you are going to get it!

Let us say, for example, that when you are out for a ride your horse decides he wants to go back to his stable. You give him a kick or two to ask him to go on, but he pays no attention. You tell yourself, "It doesn't really matter," and let him have his own way; back to the stable you go, while your horse makes up his mind that he will tell you what to do more often.

Do you really believe that, after this kind of thing has happened two or three times, giving him a lump of sugar and a pat on the neck will make him behave and do as *you* ask the next time you ride? Of course not!

The only way you are ever going to correct this is by punishment. The longer he does as he wishes, the more severe this punishment will have to be to correct him. *And it is all your fault.*

This kind of thing can be easily avoided. If you are old enough to own a horse you are old enough to be sensible. Love your horse, take good care of him, pat him, and give him tidbits—but insist, kindly but firmly, that he does as he is told.

A RELAXED ATTITUDE IS A GREAT HELP IN STAYING ON A BUCKING AND KICKING HORSE

That doesn't mean that you should give your horse a whack with a crop every time he makes a mistake or does something you don't want him to do.

It means that if your horse starts to have ideas such as turning back to the stable, immediate correction will save you untold trouble and your horse untold pain. On such a horse, be sure to carry a crop. Often the horse will cock an ear back, remember that you had a crop in your hand when you mounted, and decide to behave himself and save a lot of further trouble.

He may try to have his own way, but if you are clever you can correct him. Take your reins in one hand and your crop in the other the very instant you feel he is about to try one of his tricks, and hit him once, behind the saddle.

BUCKING. A horse will buck because of pain, such as a pinching saddle; because of a careless rider who is jabbing him in the ribs with heels or spurs; because of high-spirits from too much feed and not enough exercise; or just because he is healthy and happy and wants to tell the world about it.

Find out why he is bucking. Try to have him turned out into a paddock or pasture before you go for a ride; twenty minutes of bucking and playing by himself will "get his back down," and make him more sensible and quiet.

Don't shut him up in a stall for a day or two and expect him to go quietly when you finally get around to riding him. Try to arrange for him to be turned out in a paddock or pasture for an hour or so on the days you can't ride, especially on nice days. Cold, rainy days, of course, are no better for him than they are for you.

If he should give a buck or two while you are riding, don't worry about it! Most riders firmly believe it is difficult to stay on a bucking horse, so they promptly fall off.

If you will straighten up and stand a little in your stirrups, you will find it a lot easier to stay on. Keep your shoulders back, pull your horse's head up by quick "nips" of the reins. If you keep a steady pull, when your horse ducks his head down to buck, he will pull you right along, over his shoulder!

BALKING. A horse is said to "balk" when he stops and refuses to move forward. The very instant you feel a balker slowing down, or "coming back to you" too much, kick him sharply. If this is not enough, hit him once or twice with your crop—behind the saddle. Most balkers are just trying to find out how much you will let them get away with. If you get after them at once they will change their minds quickly.

REARING. When a horse stands up on his hind legs he is said to "rear." If a horse you are riding should rear, lean forward, loosen your reins and take hold of the mane—and sit still. Standing as he

THIS HORSE IS STARTING TO REAR AND HIS RIDER SHOULD QUICKLY LOOSEN THE REINS

is on his hind legs the horse is off balance and the slightest jerk on his mouth will make him go even higher.

While he is up in the air there is nothing you can do, but the very moment his forelegs touch the ground again, urge him forward by using your legs strongly. Keep your reins loose; it doesn't matter where he goes as long as he moves forward.

Find out at once why he reared. If you know the horse and know he does not often rear, suspect there is something wrong with his mouth. A pinching bit, a curb chain that is rough or too tight, a bad tooth, or a rough-handed rider, can make even a quiet horse rear. Try to find the cause at once, and correct it as soon as you possibly can.

Above all, never encourage your horse to rear; never buy a rearing horse, and if your horse rears often, get rid of him. No horse that rears as a habit is suitable for a young rider.

RUNNING AWAY. Running away, like many so-called vices, is often caused by the rider. If a rider hangs onto the reins or constantly nags his horse with his heels or spurs, if he allows his horse to gallop all-out across an open field, he is directly responsible for the running away.

Like bucking, running away seems worse because the rider thinks it is. Relax! If you clutch at the reins and worry, your horse will think there is really something to be afraid of, and then you *will* have trouble stopping him.

If you are in a wide field, don't try to stop him all at once. Sit up —if you lean forward you will be just asking him to gallop—and turn him in a wide circle. Keep turning him in the same direction, making your circles smaller and smaller, and soon he will become so bored with getting nowhere that he will stop.

If you can't turn him, remember that he can't run forever! Sit up. Try to raise his head with short, hard nips of the reins, but don't make the mistake of keeping up a steady pull; this will only deaden his mouth. Save your strength and then, when the horse is tired, you will still be fresh and will be able to pull him up without any further trouble.

KICKING. A horse kicks to protect himself. If he is startled by

A CHANCE TO BUCK AND PLAY IN A PADDOCK WILL MAKE A HORSE MORE QUIET TO RIDE

a sudden motion behind him, he will kick first and find out what it was later. Don't run behind a horse or touch him suddenly on the hindquarters without warning.

Horses hate to be crowded and even the quietest horse will kick if he is bumped on the quarters. Don't ride too close to the horse in front of you, and don't let anyone ride too close behind your horse; two or three horses' lengths is a good distance to keep between you.

Take warning when you see a horse put his ears back and swish his tail quickly from side to side; he is about to kick.

If your horse is a kicker, be sure to warn everyone who comes anywhere near him.

Even the sweetest-tempered horse will kick when the flies are bad; keep away from your horse's hind legs when the flies are stinging.

BITING. If your horse shows signs of biting, or nipping, don't keep taking him tidbits; horses soon learn to demand an apple or carrot this way and if there is no result they soon stop trying.

Don't fuss with your horse's head if he doesn't like it; very few horses like to be patted on the head; they much prefer to be stroked on the neck or shoulder.

If your horse does nip at you, slap him sharply on the shoulder. *Never* hit a horse on the head. One slap on the head is enough to make him head-shy; a badly head-shy horse will not allow his head to be touched and it is a definite sign of ill-treatment if a horse throws his head up when you raise your hand, even though you may only want to pat him.

SHYING. If your horse shies away from a spooky-looking object, don't snatch him in the mouth or hit him. He shied because he was suspicious of the looks of the thing; if you hurt him he will be even more convinced that there really was something to be afraid of.

Don't punish him; instead, pull up and turn to face whatever frightened him. Let him walk up to it, pat him quietly on the neck to show him there is nothing to worry about and let him put his head right down, if he wants to, to have a good look at it.

If your horse shies at a grey rock going away from the stable and then shies at it again coming back, don't think he is stupid: a horse must look at an object with *both* eyes if he is to remember it. See that you give him a chance to do this.

Every now and then you will find a horse that acts like a silly colt, bucking and shying without reason; *sometimes* this is caused by overfeeding and not enough exercise.

Try cutting down on his grain and increasing his exercise, especially by giving him about an hour a day in a pasture or paddock on days you cannot ride.

If your horse begins to lose weight and still is not quiet to ride, increase his grain at once and face your problem sensibly—your horse is too much horse for you.

Certainly you can make him behave by taking away his grain until he is sick from starvation. If you enjoy riding a tired, dull-eyed, miserable horse, then no one can stop you.

If, on the other hand, you have any real kindness, if you love your horse at all, face the facts intelligently and sell him to someone who can ride and enjoy him when he is well and happy.

It is no fun to ride a horse that is too much to handle; you will find another, more suitable—and you will be happier and get much more fun out of riding him.

IF YOUR HORSE SHOULD SHY, PULL UP AND LET HIM FACE WHATEVER FRIGHTENED HIM

Mounting and Dismounting

To mount properly, gather your reins in your left hand, standing with your back to your horse's head. If you think he might try to take a playful nip, shorten the reins on the far side a little to hold his head straight.

If you are short, or your horse is very tall, it is a good idea to lengthen your stirrup two or three holes to make mounting easier. Once you are in the saddle it is easy to shorten it again to its proper length.

Slip your left foot into the stirrup, then reach over and take hold of the far side of your saddle with your right hand. Your left hand, holding the reins, should be on your horse's neck. Give a spring with your right foot; swing your right leg over your horse's back as you turn and land gently in the saddle.

To dismount, take the reins into your left hand and take your right foot out of the stirrup. Swing your right leg over the saddle; then take your left foot out of the stirrup and drop to the ground.

Each riding rule has a very good reason behind it. Standing with your back toward your horse's head keeps you well out of the way in case the horse should try to kick. If he should start to move forward, the motion would help you swing into the saddle, instead of leaving you completely behind.

In the same way, there is a good reason for taking your left foot out of the stirrup before dropping to the ground. Some riders don't drop this stirrup until the right foot is on the ground, but this leaves them off balance for a moment, and that is always the moment when a horse decides to make a sudden move.

Make sure your horse is taught to stand still while you adjust your reins and stirrups. It is bad manners for your horse, and careless riding on your part, to let him move off before you are completely ready and have given him the signal to do so.

PREPARING TO MOUNT

MOUNTING

DISMOUNTING

YOUR HORSE CAN BE COMPLETELY UNBALANCED EVEN THOUGH HE IS STANDING QUITE STILL

The Importance of Balance

Look at the horse in the first photograph, then at the one next to it. It is the same horse and the same rider, but what a difference there is!

What is it that makes such a tremendous difference? The answer to this question is the key to all the success you will have with your riding: **Balance.**

The horse on the right is balanced; in the photograph at the left he is not.

It does seem obvious to everyone that all horses have four legs, "one at each corner," so it may seem surprising that they cannot always be properly balanced.

You may have seen horses playing in a pasture and noticed how quickly they can start, stop and turn, even at a full gallop. They are so light on their feet that they can change their speed

THE SAME HORSE, BALANCED, WITH HIS WEIGHT ON ALL FOUR LEGS, LOOKS ENTIRELY DIFFERENT

and direction in a moment. Then you find, when you are riding one of these horses, all the freedom and lightness have completely disappeared and you have to pull on the reins to get him to turn at all!

This unpleasant feeling is due to your horse's lack of balance. When you get on his back your horse's first idea is to take your extra weight in the laziest way he can, no matter how light you may be. If you allow him to do so, he will carry this weight on his shoulders and front legs, or *forehand,* as this is called by horsemen.

A well-balanced horse carries his weight on *all four legs;* not just on his forehand, but on his hind legs as well. This is terribly important, because all of a horse's power in turning, jumping, moving forward, and stopping comes from his hind legs. A balanced

THIS WELL-BALANCED HORSE IS STOPPING SUDDENLY, WITH HIS WEIGHT ON HIS HIND LEGS

horse has his hind legs well underneath his body so he can use them to turn or stop at once. An unbalanced horse moves on his forehand, with his hind legs following along, not in any position to be of any help at all.

This may seem to be a lot of fuss about a complicated thing, but you must realize that even the very best horse cannot do *anything* well if he is not balanced. **An unbalanced horse is always the sign of a poor or careless rider.**

YOUR POSITION IN THE SADDLE

First of all, let's check the length of your stirrups. The stirrup irons themselves should be large and heavy. They should be about an inch wider than the ball of your foot. A larger iron would let your foot slip all the way through, which would be dangerous; you must always be able to pull your foot out of the stirrup easily in case you take a tumble. For the same reason, your stirrup irons should not be too narrow.

A good way to test the length of your stirrups is to have the lower edge of the iron just tapping your ankle bone when you sit relaxed in the saddle with your legs hanging down straight. They should not be more than one hole longer than this, as you would then have to keep reaching down for them, throwing the rest of your body off balance.

Forget any ideas you may have that knee grip alone is important. Your security in the saddle comes through balance, and the grip you need you will achieve by a proper position.

Stand up in your stirrups (don't use your hands to balance yourself) and let all your weight sink down through the back of your legs to your heels, forcing them down. Then sit straight down, well toward the front of the saddle. This will put the upper part of

TESTING LENGTH OF STIRRUP

THIS IS A GOOD EXAMPLE OF CORRECT HORSEMANSHIP AND A NICELY BALANCED HORSE

your leg close against the saddle, and you will feel this contact from your hip to a point just below your knee.

Let your ankles relax. If you have the stirrup iron on the ball of your foot, and have your foot placed as close as you can get it to the inner side of the iron—the side toward the girth—your ankle will "break away" at a comfortable angle.

Now your legs are in a position to give you all the grip you need. If you should make the mistake of trying to grip with your knees alone you will tire very quickly. The result will be that your heels will fly up and you will start to grip with the back, or calves of your legs. This will force you up out of the saddle in a very uncomfortable way and if you are on a horse with any spirit at all, this constant pressure of your calves against his sides will make him fuss and fidget all the time.

Sit up straight. Relax your back, but keep your shoulders square and your chin up. Look straight ahead between your horse's ears; this will keep that unattractive hump out of your back without stiffness. Your back must be able to "give" with every stride of your horse.

I have left the position of your hands until the last because you cannot have good hands without a balanced, secure seat. Good hands will come only when you have learned to keep your proper position. You must, of course, always ride with both hands on the reins. Riding with one hand not only twists your whole body, but it gives you only half control of your horse.

Your reins—and your hands through the reins—signal your horse to turn and stop, and, most important of all, they balance your horse with soft, light pressure on the bit. You cannot do any of this unless your hands work together as a pair.

Relax your arms right down to your elbows; this will keep them close to your sides in an easy, natural position. If you tense your shoulders and arms, your elbows will fly away from your sides, which does not look well and completely spoils your hands.

The hands themselves should be held a few inches apart with the wrists relaxed and turned to put them in the same position as those of the girl in the photograph.

This is where your hands belong. Never spread them far apart to turn your horse. Your hands belong together at all times.

One more important thing to remember: Keep your left hand on the left side of your horse's neck; your right hand on the right side. Your hands must never, at any time, cross over from one side to the other.

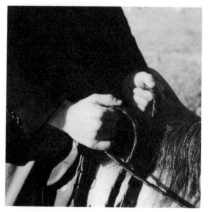
CORRECT WAY OF HOLDING SINGLE REINS

CORRECT WAY OF HOLDING DOUBLE REINS

RIDER'S CARELESS HORSEMANSHIP CAN PUT EVEN A WELL-SCHOOLED HORSE OFF BALANCE

The Walk

Compare these two photographs. The reason the horse on the left looks straggled and sloppy is that he is unbalanced. The photograph at the right is of the same horse and rider—balanced.

All balance and smartness in the way your horse moves are brought about by a partnership between your legs and hands. Your horse uses his head and neck a great deal to balance himself; it is easy to understand that if your horse's head is carried low it pitches his weight forward onto his forehand. You don't want him to be on his forehand, so the answer should be obvious; your horse must carry his head up to be balanced.

To balance your horse: Make sure there is always an upward slope from his withers to his ears, by squeezing him strongly with the calves of your legs. (Don't turn your knees out as you do this. Your knees must stay flat against the saddle. It is not the backs of your calves that you use, but the inside muscles of your legs.)

THE HORSE IS ALERT AND WELL-BALANCED WHEN THE SAME PERSON RIDES HIM PROPERLY

At the same time your reins must be short enough to give you light contact with your horse's mouth. This means that with soft, relaxed wrists you can feel the bit through the reins. In this way, as the pressure of your legs raises your horse's head and urges him forward, your hands steady him quietly—and you have a balanced horse.

To go into a walk from a standstill, adjust your reins to the proper length and give your horse a squeeze with the lower part of your legs.

With some horses only a light touch of your heels is enough as a signal to increase pace or to turn. With others, however, their sides have not been trained to respond to this pressure, so you may have to squeeze quite hard.

Some horses have never been thoroughly trained, or schooled, as this is called by horsemen. Remember that you will be signaling these horses in a strange language that they do not understand. If your horse is like this you will have to use very strong leg pressure at first, but gradually, as you ride, you can school him to respond to the lightest touch. This is worth working for.

Make sure your horse walks along at a brisk pace by squeezing with your legs whenever he begins to lag. It will keep him balanced and alert.

This is the reason for having your legs back underneath you as you do in the forward seat; they are then always in the position to be used properly.

You will notice that, as your horse walks, he bobs his head up and down with each stride. If your arms and hands are relaxed, as they should be, they will move slightly, back and forth, with this bobbing. If you "freeze" your arms and wrists, stiffening them so there is no "give" to them at all, you will find that your horse may lean on the bit, pulling and fussing and tossing his head. The steady pressure of frozen wrists and hands is annoying, sometimes painful to your horse. Keep checking on your position in the

THIS RIDER IS DEMONSTRATING THE WRONG WAY OF TURNING HORSE BY PULLING ON REINS

saddle; if you are relaxed, your hands will improve enormously.

Turning your horse is done the same way at all times, but it is best to practice this at a walk until you can do it correctly.

In all your turns be sure that your horse's head, neck, shoulders, and body stay in a straight line.

You so often see a horse being turned like this: First the rider's hand is put out to the side, pulling on the rein. The horse turns his head, following the direction of the pull; then his neck turns, then his shoulders and body bend in a curve until his hind legs follow along. Nothing could look more awkward and uncomfortable.

This is the correct way to turn your horse in a circle to the left:

Your left hand increases the pressure of the rein slightly to guide him to the left. Your right hand, surprisingly enough, is going to do most of the turning, by increasing its pressure and pressing the right rein aganst your horse's neck. Don't forget that his head and neck must stay in a straight line. Keep your hands together.

THE CORRECT METHOD OF TURNING A HORSE IS TO USE YOUR HANDS AND LEGS TOGETHER

As your hands guide him on the turn to the left, your right leg is drawn back slightly where you press it firmly against his side, behind the girth.

Your left leg is quite still, but be ready to use it to keep him moving on.

Remember: Your hands guide and control the forehand (head, neck, shoulders and forelegs).

Your legs also guide your horse; the left leg, drawn back and pressed against his side makes him move away from the pressure, to the right.

The right leg, drawn back and pressed against his side, moves his body and hindquarters away from the pressure to the left.

Both legs squeezing behind the girth make your horse bring his hind legs under him where he can use them properly, and urge him forward.

Here is a photograph that illustrates two very important points; balance and horsemanship. This horse is shying away from an object which frightened him; notice that in his quick, natural motion he is turning *on his hind legs;* his front hoofs aren't touching the ground. To balance himself quickly to turn like this, he threw his head higher. The rider's hands are down, to lower his head. Her left leg is drawn back and her heel is pressing against his side to stop him from moving further to the left. In a moment, as soon as the horse straightens, her legs together will urge the horse forward again.

No one can pose a photograph like this, as no one could possibly think fast enough to use her hands and legs correctly in an instant. This rider didn't have to think because she had worked hard on her horsemanship, and learned the proper use of hands and legs. Then, at a time when this could be of real help to her, it was a perfectly natural and immediate reaction to use her hands and legs as she should. There can be no stronger reason for learning good horsemanship.

SHYING HORSE USES HIND
LEGS TO STOP AND TO TURN

Backing

To make your horse back up, first have him standing squarely on all four legs. In other words, have him balanced. Shorten your reins a little, then give a light squeeze with your legs as though you were about to ask him to move into a walk.

Instead of letting him take a step, gently increase the pressure on the reins. Squeeze with your legs just behind the girth and your horse will back up.

Keep your hands down.

Always make your horse back in a straight line. If he starts to turn as he backs, don't forget that the pressure of a single leg will straighten his hindquarters. If he starts to curve to the left, use your left leg. Stop the pressure as soon as he straightens.

Have him back about four steps, then relax the pressure of the reins, move your legs a little farther back, and squeeze to urge him forward again. Walk forward a few steps and stop. Have him stand still for a moment, loosen your reins and pat him, before you move on again.

Don't practice backing too much at one time.

Try to have your horse back without throwing his head into the air or bending his neck too much. The horse in this photograph is being backed correctly; his lower jaw is relaxed, giving to the light pressure of the bit, and his head is at a normal angle.

BACKING CORRECTLY; THE HORSE'S HEAD IS IN THE PROPER POSITION, WITH MOUTH CLOSED

A TROTTING HORSE CAN BE EASILY THROWN OFF BALANCE BY CARELESS HORSEMANSHIP

The Trot

A balanced horse has a free, smart trot, with a definite one-two, one-two beat. A horse off balance, either because he is allowed to carry his weight on his forehand, or because he is forced to trot faster than he can, will go into a rapid one-two-three-four patter.

To say that a horse is trotting "faster than he can" certainly sounds odd, but it is possible. You know you can walk at a certain speed. If you are told to go faster, your walk will get little hops and skips in it, even though it is still called a walk.

The same is true of your horse. There is a certain speed at which he can trot in a balanced, smooth stride. Find out how fast this is, then never let him trot any faster. Forcing his speed beyond his natural limit is a strain on him and uncomfortable for you; you will find your riding has lost all its smoothness.

To make him trot at his best, squeeze him strongly with your legs to urge him forward, while your hands steady and balance him.

SMOOTH HORSEMANSHIP AND GOOD, QUIET HANDS STEADY HORSE BACK INTO BALANCE

As your horse trots, his hoofs hit the ground in that one-two, one-two beat. At one beat his left foreleg and his right hind leg move forward and hit the ground together. On the second beat his right foreleg and his left hind leg hit the ground in another stride.

As your horse trots you rise and sink back into the saddle in rhythm with his stride; this is called posting.

At the trot be sure you are sitting well forward in the saddle, with your legs back underneath you. As you post let every stride push your weight down through your heels.

Don't pump when you post! You so often see riders heaving themselves up and down when they are trotting. How silly this looks, because it is so unnecessary! Instead of throwing himself up into the air when he posts, a horseman lets the horse do all the work.

With each trotting stride your horse gives a strong thrust with his hind leg. Let this thrust push you out of the saddle, then sink

[51]

as that leg goes back. Try to see how *little* you have to rise out of the saddle. You will be surprised at how much smoother this feels, and I can't tell you how much smoother it will make your horsemanship look!

Your horse's head does not bob up and down at the trot as it does when he is walking. You won't have to let your hands move back and forth with each stride. You will, however, have to be sure your hands don't move up and down as you post; they should keep quite still. This means you will have to relax your arms and hands so your elbows can bend as you post.

To break smoothly into a trot from a walk, have your horse walking briskly with his head up. Don't work so hard at this that your poor horse has to carry his head stuck up into the air! If you find that your horse is beginning to get his head up too high, it is your fault. You are grabbing hold of his mouth with your reins too short, thinking that you have "contact." It isn't a nice, light contact at all. Loosen your reins and let his head drop down to a comfortable position.

When your horse is walking well, shorten your reins a little, remembering not to overdo it, and squeeze with both legs behind the girth. *Sit still* to the first few trotting strides, until your horse has settled into a good, even trot, then quietly begin to post. If you

POSTING ON THE RIGHT DIAGONAL, RISING AS THE RIGHT FORELEG MOVES FORWARD – –

should start to post as soon as the horse breaks into a trot you will throw him off balance as you will be heaving up and down in a very odd rhythm while he settles into his stride.

You will find that if your horse likes to rush off into a trot, this way of breaking him into it will help a great deal.

DIAGONALS

As explained in the beginning of this chapter, when a horse trots, the foreleg on one side and the hind leg on the other side move together in one stride.

When you post, you rise as one foreleg reaches out, and sink in the saddle as the same foreleg comes back. If you rise as the right foreleg goes out and sink as it comes back, you are said to be posting on the right *diagonal,* as the rider in these photographs is doing.

In the beginning you can tell which diagonal you are on by looking down at your horse's shoulder. You will see it move and can check on your diagonals this way.

Horses are like people. They each have a "hand" they prefer, just as you are either right- or left-handed. If your horse prefers his right "hand" he will try to make you post on the right diagonal. If

-- AND SINKING INTO THE SADDLE AS THE RIGHT FORELEG AND SHOULDER MOVE BACK

you haven't known about diagonals you may never have noticed this, but you can be sure your horse has been putting you on the diagonal he prefers.

Trot a few strides, long enough to decide which diagonal you are on, then walk, then trot again. The chances are you are right back on the same diagonal—because your horse has put you there.

To change your diagonal while you are trotting, post along for a few strides, then sit in your saddle to miss one stride and quickly start posting again. Check with your horse's shoulder and if you have done this correctly, you will have changed diagonals.

The chances are you will know right away because it may be very uncomfortable. This is because the muscles on the diagonal your horse doesn't want you to use have not been developed and strengthened as much as on the side he prefers. For this reason diagonals are important; posting on both diagonals develops the horse's shoulder muscles on both sides.

When you are trotting in a circle or in a ring, the correct diagonal is the one on the outside of the circle. If you are trotting in a circle to the right you must be on the left diagonal. Trotting in a circle to the left, you must be on the right diagonal.

Good riders don't have to look down at their horse's shoulder to see which diagonal they are on. You will have to do this at first, of course, but after you have practiced for a while, try to get the feeling of diagonals. In a surprisingly short time you will be able to break your horse into a trot and start posting on the correct diagonal without having to look down at all.

Practice your diagonals and balance by trotting in a figure eight. Break into a trot, remembering to sit still to those first few strides, and circle to the left, posting on the right diagonal. Make a complete circle, and when you have reached the point where you started, change diagonals and circle to the right on the left diagonal.

Figure eights are wonderful practice for you and your horse. Remember to keep his head, neck and back in a straight line; don't separate your hands as you turn, and be sure to use your legs properly. Make your circles large enough so your horse doesn't trot in a cramped, uncomfortable way.

When you want to slow from a trot to a walk, don't just lean back and pull. Instead, increase the pressure on the reins slightly, with your hands down. The very instant you feel your horse starting to respond, give to him by loosening the reins a little. Sit down in your saddle and stop posting and your horse will slow to a free and balanced walk.

If you hear a sharp clicking sound as your horse trots, your horse is striking the toe of his front hoof with the toe of his hind hoof at every stride. This is called "forging."

A horse may forge because he is off balance; if you are letting him go along on his forehand, he is not getting his foreleg off the ground soon enough. If you are quite sure, however, that your horse is balanced and he still forges, it is the fault of his shoeing.

Horses' feet are growing all the time. If the hoofs are not pared down every four or six weeks, the toes will grow so long that your horse may stumble—or forge when he trots.

Have your horse's feet checked every month. If the shoes are not worn out the blacksmith will take them off, pare the hoof down to its proper length, and replace them. Don't wait until the shoes are completely worn out; letting your horse go too long without having his hoofs cared for puts a terrible strain on his legs.

FORGING: THE TOE OF THIS HORSE'S HIND SHOE WILL STRIKE THE TOE OF HIS FOREHOOF

The Canter

The canter is a slow, collected gallop. Before discussing your position, it is important for you to understand cantering *leads*.

Watch your horse as he is cantering loose in a field, or watch a horse being ridden by another person. If you look carefully you will see that, as he canters, one foreleg reaches farther out than the other with each stride.

If the left foreleg reaches farther out, the horse is on the left lead; if it is the right leg, the horse is on the right lead.

Leads support your horse's weight as he turns at a canter. If he turns to the left he must be on the left lead to keep his balance. Therefore, when you turn a corner or canter in a circle, the leg toward the inside of the circle must be leading. (This is just the opposite of diagonals.)

You will soon find that with a little practice it will be easy for you to tell which lead your horse is on as you canter. It is even easier to tell this from the ground, at first, so if you are not quite sure, ask someone to help you by watching as you canter.

Decide for yourself which lead you think you are on, then make sure you are right by asking your helper. In a very short time you will always be right and soon you will be able to tell without looking at all, just by the feeling of the way your horse moves.

You know when you canter in a circle that the leg toward the inside of the circle must be leading, so the next thing to find out is how to make your horse take the correct lead. A well-balanced horse will often do this without the help of his rider, but not always, so it is important for you to give him the proper signal *each time* you go into a canter.

CANTERING ON LEFT LEAD, LEFT FORELEG EXTENDS FARTHER THAN THE RIGHT AT EACH STRIDE

Always go into a canter from a walk. Then you will be sure your horse is balanced. Not only is that important, but cantering from a walk schools your horse to obey your legs and it shows that both you and your horse know what you are doing and how to do it properly.

To put your horse on the correct lead—let's say you want to be on the left lead—have him walking along briskly. Shorten your reins quietly and, if he is a sleepy kind of a horse, squeeze him strongly with your legs to let him know he must be ready.

Turn his whole body slightly to the right by increasing the pressure on the right rein just a little. At the same time, press your right leg strongly behind the girth.

Your horse knows that you want him to go forward because you told him so with your legs and hands before giving the cantering signals. Then, when you turn him slightly to the right and use your right leg he will move away from this pressure to the left and forward at the same time—by breaking into a canter on the left lead.

Your left leg stays quite still, and your left hand is used only to steady your horse and to keep his head straight.

Don't make the mistake of kicking or squeezing with both legs as you ask your horse to go into a canter; that is the signal to trot. You use only *one* leg to signal for a canter; the leg opposite the lead you want your horse to take.

You may find at first that your horse either goes into a very fast trot or takes the wrong lead. This is because you haven't used your hands and legs properly. Pull him up quietly, let him walk a few steps, then try again. If he still goes off at a trot, go back to balance. Keep a light feel of his mouth as he walks and when you give him the signal to canter, don't let him trot! Keep your hands down and don't post; if you do, you are just asking him to trot. Sit down in the saddle, keep a light but firm touch on the reins, and he will finally understand and do as you ask.

A well-schooled horse, well ridden, will go from a walk into a canter without taking a single trotting stride.

Don't throw your body forward, raise your hands or swing your legs about when you go into a canter. The only thing you achieve by doing this is to throw your horse off balance. All your signals to your horse should be as quiet as you can possibly make them.

As you canter, let your weight sink down through the backs of your legs to your heels. Lean very slightly forward against the increase in speed and keep your legs still. Your reins should be a little shorter at the canter than at the walk or trot. Your horse's

CORRECT HORSEMANSHIP AT THE CANTER; RIDER IS IN GOOD POSITION, HORSE BALANCED

head will nod a bit with each stride, so your shoulders, arms and wrists must be relaxed to allow your hands to move a little with this motion. Keep your head up and look ahead.

Canter slowly, always. Any horse can gallop; only a balanced horse, well-ridden, can canter slowly, quietly and smoothly.

Never canter your horse, or ride at a fast trot, on a paved road, through mud, or over rough and stony ground. The tiny bones in your horse's hoofs and the muscles and tendons in his legs can easily be damaged by the shock of hitting a hard, ungiving surface at speed. Mud clings to your horse's legs and if you force him through it faster than a walk he may only lose one of his shoes; on the other hand, he may pull a tendon. The weeks of lameness that follow a strained tendon will teach you to ride slowly through mud, but why wait until this happens?

To pull your horse up from a canter to a walk, straighten and sit down in your saddle. Keep your hands down as you gently increase the pressure of the reins. As soon as you feel your horse coming back to you and slowing, give to him by relaxing your pull and he will drop back into a walk.

Figure eights are excellent cantering practice. Break your horse onto his left lead from a walk. If he takes even one trotting stride, pull up and start again. Canter in a circle to the left.

When you have made a complete circle, pull up to a walk and break off on the right lead, circling to the right. Remember to use your legs as well as your hands on the turns.

Another good exercise is to break your horse off on the left lead and canter several strides in a straight line. Stop, remembering to sit up and to keep your hands down. Back four steps, walk forward four steps, and break off on the right lead. This is an excellent exercise for a horse that likes to canter too fast or that leans on the bit.

Why is this such a good exercise for a horse that pulls and carries his head too low?

Because the stopping and backing raises his head, takes weight off his forehand, and brings his hind legs under his body to balance him.

AN EXAMPLE OF QUIET HANDS AND EXCELLENT HORSEMANSHIP: PULLING UP FROM A CANTER

The Hand-Gallop

When you have learned to balance your horse and to ride smoothly at the walk, trot, and canter, the next step is the hand-gallop.

The hand-gallop is not a new, different gait; it is an extended canter. With the increase in speed your horse will take longer strides and move with his body down a little closer to the ground.

You have probably galloped your horse more than once, letting him run as fast as he wanted to across a field with your reins flying loose. Surely by now you realize that you should not ride this way.

Suppose you ride into a field or a long lane and turn your horse's head loose for a nice gallop. Your horse flies off as fast as he can go and you make no effort to hold him back.

Suddenly you catch sight of a hole in the ground a few feet in front of you. Your horse is completely unbalanced. To keep your horse from stepping into the hole you probably know by now what you would have to do.

First you must shorten your reins. Then you must change your position, sitting up and getting down into your saddle. Then you must raise your horse's head—not always an easy thing to do—to take the weight off his forehand, then bring his quarters underneath him so he can turn.

All this takes time—too much time. How much better it would have been if you had never let your horse become unbalanced in the first place!

A hand-gallop is a *controlled* gallop. A horseman never lets his horse run as fast as he can for two very good reasons.

First, a horse running at all-out speed is out of control. A horseman never lets this happen because then the rider is only a passenger, without the power to do anything at all in case of an emergency.

The second reason is that a horse's legs are surprisingly delicate. One wild gallop can do more harm to your horse than hours of slower, considerate riding. The strain of all-out speed is unbelievably hard on every muscle and tendon in your horse's body.

Of course, race horses are ridden as fast as they can go; but race horses are given months of special, careful training to get them fit and ready before they race. Their trainers know what damage can be done by the strain of speed on a horse not racing fit.

GOOD HAND-GALLOP POSITION: HEAD UP, SHOULDERS SQUARE, HANDS AND HEELS DOWN

Your horse will never be as fit as a race horse and so he must never be asked to gallop as fast as he can go.

YOUR POSITION AT THE HAND-GALLOP

After you have exercised your horse for half an hour or so to settle him down, put him into a canter. When he is cantering along nicely, rise out of your saddle a little and move your hands down and forward, as the girl in this photograph is doing. This will put your body a little further forward than it has been before. Shorten your reins; let your weight sink through your legs, down through your heels. Be sure the stirrup iron is on the ball of your foot so your ankle will bend and allow your heels to go down.

Do not lean on your hands. You must learn to hold this position without their help. Don't stiffen your body; relax as much as you can. Look ahead.

Hold this position, riding as quietly and as easily as you can, until you begin to get tired. Then have your horse walk. After you have rested, try it again while cantering on the other lead.

You won't be able to hold the galloping position very long at a time when you first try it. Take your time and get used to it gradually; don't try to keep it up when you are tired. You will begin to ride sloppily and learn bad horsemanship that will be hard to forget.

Be sure to keep your horse at a steady, ordinary canter while you practice, for two reasons. First, your horse can canter for a much longer time than he can gallop, without tiring, giving you more of a chance to practice. Secondly, it teaches you to keep your own balance as you learn to use your hands and legs, before you go on to a faster pace.

When you can keep up out of your saddle and have gotten the rhythm of this forward position; when you can move your hands and legs to guide and control your horse without disturbing your own balance, you are ready to go on to the true hand-gallop.

Canter a bit in the galloping position, then urge your horse to go slightly faster by increasing the pressure of your legs and giving to him a little more with your hands. If this is properly done, your horse will be galloping at a pace slightly faster than a canter, moving steadily and quietly, still feeling balanced and responsive. If he is not, it is your fault; you haven't learned to balance and control him in this position. Work a little more on your horsemanship.

An excellent exercise at the hand-gallop is to start off at a slow, collected canter, riding in the galloping position. Increase your speed gradually and smoothly into a hand-gallop.

After galloping along a few moments, ease your horse back into a canter, without changing your position more than is absolutely necessary. You will have to sit up a little more, but be sure to stay up out of your saddle.

After you have cantered several strides, send your horse gradually into a gallop again.

This exercise is very good for your horsemanship as it teaches you control. It is also important for two other reasons.

Your horse learns that just because you are riding in the galloping position doesn't mean you expect him to change his pace or fly off at a run. He learns that he must wait for your signals. A horse that begins to fret and pull as soon as his rider "gets forward" shows that he has been poorly schooled.

This exercise also will help you to control your horse smoothly when you start jumping. You will, at some time, want to jump several fences with turns and up- and down-hill slopes in between them. If, before you start this kind of jumping, your horse has been taught to go from a canter to a smooth hand-gallop and back to a canter again, you have already won half the battle toward an even, polished jumping performance.

To pull up from a gallop, straighten and sit down in your saddle. As you do this, you will have to raise your hands to their normal position. Steady your horse quietly and he will come back to you. Don't post if he should take a few trotting strides before dropping into a walk.

One more word—and an important one—about the gallop. **Never gallop your horse around a sharp corner.** Even though you are riding well, and your horse is under control, no matter how clever he may be, he cannot turn a sharp corner at that speed. He cannot keep his balance and he will fall.

When you are galloping and approaching a turn, or the narrow end of a ring, straighten a little and slow down. The rider in this photograph is starting to turn her horse to the left. She is still up out of her saddle with her weight balanced and driven down through her heels; her hands are light and steady on the reins. The horse is, of course, on the left lead.

Once you are around the turn, gradually move into a gallop again. This proves once more the importance of teaching yourself and your horse to change pace smoothly.

GOOD HORSEMANSHIP; STEADYING AND SLOWING THE HORSE TO TURN AT THE HAND-GALLOP

How Your Horse Jumps

Of course you want to jump. Everyone does. Jumping is fun, from the very beginning; from the first moment when you pop your horse over a low rail and feel the satisfaction of having jumped *with* your horse instead of just being a passenger. Every fence you jump from then on will teach you something new and will add an even greater pleasure to your riding.

Before you can become more than a passenger on a jumping horse, no matter how much experience you may have had, it is very important that you know and understand *how* a horse jumps.

Remember, as you look at the following photographs, that your horse feels the same way about jumping as you do; he wants to approach the fence smoothly, jump it safely and easily, and land on the far side still balanced and in his stride. Notice how the horse in the photographs uses his head and neck to balance himself.

Remember, too: Your forward seat horsemanship will allow full freedom to your horse's natural motions and balance while you are in the position to aid, guide and control him.

HORSE APPROACHES FENCE WITH HEAD UP, EARS PRICKED, JUDGING HEIGHT AND WIDTH. HE IS ALERT, BALANCED

HE CHECKS SLIGHTLY, BRINGING HIND LEGS FORWARD; HEAD AND NECK MOVE DOWN AND FORWARD AS HE TAKES OFF

IN THE AIR OVER THE FENCE HIS HEAD AND NECK REACH OUT; FORELEGS ARE FOLDED TO AVOID HITTING FENCE

AT FAR SIDE OF FENCE HE BEGINS TO RAISE HIS HEAD; HIS FORELEGS ARE UNFOLDING AS HE TUCKS UP HIND LEGS

HEAD AND NECK SLIGHTLY RAISED BUT
STILL EXTENDED; ONE FORELEG WILL HIT
GROUND AN INSTANT BEFORE THE OTHER

BOTH FORELEGS HAVE LANDED; HEAD STILL
EXTENDED; IN A MOMENT HIS HIND LEGS
WILL LAND AND HORSE WILL CANTER ON

APPROACH IN HAND-GALLOP POSITION;
NEAR FENCE PUT HANDS WELL FORWARD

Jumping Horsemanship

If you have been jumping without paying much attention to your horsemanship, it would be a very good idea for you to start again, working on your horsemanship over low fences.

If you are just starting to jump, no matter how low your first fence may be, it may look difficult unless you remember this: Your horse's jump over a low fence is nothing more than an extra-long cantering stride. If you keep this in mind you won't think jumping is so difficult, and you will be quite right.

You can't expect your horse just to carry you along over a fence. The most important thing for you to learn as you start jumping is to jump *with* your horse. Learn to get forward and to go with him; throw your mind and your heart over the fence, and you and your horse will follow together.

AS HORSE TAKES OFF, PUSH YOURSELF
FORWARD; HEAD UP, SHOULDERS SQUARE

HOLD THIS POSITION IN THE AIR; LET YOUR
WEIGHT SINK DOWN THROUGH YOUR HEELS

AS YOUR HORSE LANDS, KEEP UP OUT OF THE SADDLE, HANDS AND HEELS DOWN

STAY OUT OF THE SADDLE AND CANTER ON IN SAME HAND-GALLOP POSITION

You can see in these photographs that this rider is never down in her saddle, from the approach through the recovery. Stay up out of your saddle in the forward hand-gallop position all through your jump; pretend the back of your saddle has been cut away.

Practice over and over again, over low fences, until you never flop back into the saddle, or until you never get "left behind."

When a rider does get left behind, it is hard on the horse for two reasons. First, the weight suddenly coming down on his back will make him drop his hind legs and rap the fence, which he doesn't want to do; secondly, the rider's hands are bound to jerk back and yank the horse in the mouth.

Nothing bothers a horse more than not being able to use his head and neck freely to balance himself as he jumps. You must be absolutely sure to put your hands up and allow your horse enough free rein as he jumps to give him this freedom.

THIS HORSE COULD NOT EXTEND HIS HEAD ENOUGH AS THE REINS WERE A LITTLE TOO TIGHT

ONE JAB IN THE MOUTH CAN VERY QUICKLY SPOIL A HORSE'S CONFIDENCE IN HIS RIDER

The girl on the grey horse in the photograph on the left was left behind and is jerking her horse in the mouth. You can see that this horse, because he threw his head up from the sudden pain, is going to drop his hind legs and rap the top rail quite hard. Horses don't forget things like this very quickly; and it will be some time before this horse trusts his rider again.

Don't let this happen to you. A horse must jump with confidence in himself and his rider if he is to jump freely and well. If he is afraid of his mouth being jerked, or afraid that his rider will not give him enough free rein to use his head and neck, he *cannot* jump well.

Never make a habit of holding onto the mane. However, if you are not absolutely sure of yourself or of your horse, it is better to hold onto the mane than to take the chance of being caught off balance and jerking your horse's mouth.

The more jumping experience you have, the less you will need to hold onto the mane; though even good riders will do it every once in a while.

This is a photograph of a very good rider on a bold, free jumper. The horse put in a big jump over this fence and the rider was slightly left behind—but she quickly took hold of the mane. The reins are still loose enough, and the horse is relaxed with a comfortable, free head.

THOUGH SLIGHTLY "LEFT" RIDER AVOIDED JERKING THE HORSE'S MOUTH BY HOLDING MANE

Advanced Jumping

You have learned that until you have complete confidence in yourself and in your horse, you must let him alone as he jumps. You have also learned to approach and jump a fence staying up out of the saddle; your weight sinking through your heels with the upper part of your legs close against the saddle; your head up, your shoulders square, and your hands giving your horse his head.

Now you are ready to do even more.

The only real change you make in your horsemanship as you advance in experience and good horsemanship is to follow through the motions of your horse's head and neck with your hands. Instead of placing them up on his horse's neck, a good rider lets his hands move *down* and *forward* as he jumps; notice in the following photographs that not only do this rider's hands follow through beautifully, but that there is also always a straight line from his elbows, through his hands and the reins to the horse's bit.

RIDER APPROACHES THE FENCE IN HAND-GALLOP POSITION, WITH HIS HORSE WELL BALANCED

AS THE HORSE TAKES OFF, RIDER GOES FORWARD SMOOTHLY, LEGS STILL, HEELS WELL DOWN

DURING FLIGHT, THE RIDER'S HANDS MOVE TO FOLLOW THE MOTIONS OF HIS HORSE'S HEAD

IN FLIGHT BOTH ARE BALANCED, RIDER KEEPING A LIGHT CONTACT WITH HIS HORSE'S MOUTH

THE HORSE LANDS WITH THE RIDER STILL UP OUT OF SADDLE, LOOKING AHEAD, HANDS DOWN

THE RIDER IS STILL IN A BALANCED HAND-GALLOP POSITION AS HIS HORSE CANTERS ON

Horsemanship like this is not luck and it doesn't just happen by itself. It is the result of hours of patient practice; practice in doing the right thing at the right time, over and over again. This is not said to discourage you; if you are that easily discouraged, you would give up too soon, anyway. It is just to emphasize the fact that you mustn't expect to be able to ride like this without working at it—and the results are well worth the effort!

It takes only one sharp jerk in the mouth to spoil your horse's free, bold way of jumping.

The speed, or *pace* at which you ride toward a fence is important. If your horse heaves himself up over the fence, it doesn't take much imagination to tell you that your pace was too slow.

On the other hand, dashing helter-skelter at a fence will not be much better. Extreme speed puts your horse off-balance, onto his forehand. When he reaches the fence he must either throw himself over it as well as he can, which won't be very well; or put in two or three sudden short strides to check himself and get his weight back onto his hindquarters. These jolting strides are uncomfortable for both you and the horse.

A horse can jump a low fence from a stand-still.

A horse can jump a slightly higher fence, very comfortably, from a trot. Practice trotting over low fences; it is very good for your horsemanship.

To have your horse jump smoothly at a good pace, however, you must work on your *timing*. Timing is knowing exactly when your horse will take off at a fence, and being able to judge the last few strides before the fence.

Watch other horses jumping. As you do, try to count their last three strides before they take off. Count to yourself *one—two—three;* and, if your timing was correct, the horse will rise off the ground on the count of *three.*

Try this while you are jumping yourself. Keep working at it until you are right almost every jump. Keep working at it until you can time every fence correctly, whether you are jumping or watching someone else jump.

Once you have learned timing your jumping will improve enormously.

To jump well your horse should lengthen his stride smoothly as he comes near the fence. To have him do this, always start toward a fence at a controlled canter, increasing your speed gradually. Give to your horse with your hands by letting them move down and forward just a little so that on the count of *one* he will lengthen his stride a bit. On the count of *two* his stride should lengthen again, very slightly; and on the count of *three* he will take off in a beautiful, free jump that will make you feel there isn't a fence in the world too big for you.

Sometimes, however, though you think your pace and timing were right, your horse will suddenly put in a short, extra stride before taking off. This is called "getting under a fence" and it feels very awkward.

A horse will do this for a number of reasons. You may have missed your timing without realizing it and asked your horse to take off while he was still too far away from the fence; a clever horse will put in a short stride rather than take any chances.

A horse will refuse to jump for the same reasons he may have for putting in that short, extra stride. Here are some of the questions you should ask yourself if your horse is getting under his fences, or refusing to jump at all:

Have you been jumping too much? Jumping the same fence over and over again or jumping a great number of fences every

WHEN A HORSE REFUSES TO JUMP, IT IS IMPORTANT FOR THE RIDER TO FIND THE REASON

day will turn a horse sour because he becomes tired and bored. Use a little common sense; don't overdo your jumping.

Is he afraid of you? If you have not been giving him a free head, your horse will be afraid to extend his head and neck because of the jerk in the mouth he soon learns to expect. You will have to regain his confidence in you before he will jump well again.

Is he lame? A lame horse must *never* be asked to jump. The pain of landing on a sore leg will very soon ruin a good jumper.

Are you quite sure you wanted to jump that fence? A hesitant rider who hangs back, even the least bit, from jumping a fence, cannot fool his horse. The horse feels this, starts to worry, and puts in a hesitant jump himself. If you ride at a fence, go on and jump it with every thought, every intention of flying over it. If you are worried about the height, lower it! If you have the sense to be worried about the mud on the take-off side, don't jump it!

Don't jump out of mud or off rough or stony ground.

Don't walk over wire; don't ever jump a fence with wire in front of it or over it; keep away from wire at all times.

Don't jump a fence unless you are sure the take-off is on good, firm ground and that the landing is the same, free from holes or anything that might trip your horse.

It is far better to take the time to walk your horse up to a strange fence and check it over carefully, than to be sorry later.

Don't jump out onto a hard road unless it is absolutely necessary. If you do have to, then just pop your horse over the fence at a very slow pace. Hard roads are slippery.

If you are following another horse over a fence, be sure to keep a safe "hunting distance" between you. A safe distance is two or three lengths more than you intended to keep; you must be able to stop your horse safely in case the horse in front of you refuses, or loses his rider on the landing side.

A hard hat, such as a hunt cap, is excellent protection; wear one when you jump. You have probably noticed that every rider on a jumping horse throughout this book is wearing a hunt cap.

To avoid a refusal when you know one is coming, go on into your fence strongly, hold your horse straight at it; if you feel him dropping back, slowing and coming back to you, squeeze him strongly with your legs those last three strides.

If your horse swerves and runs around a jump, he is said to have "run out." A run-out is the result of careless horsemanship. You can't always help having a refusal, but you should always be awake and ready with your hands and legs to keep your horse from running out.

Never punish a horse for refusing by jerking him in the mouth. If you don't know the reason for this by now, you had better go back and read these chapters on jumping all over again.

It is important to keep up out of your saddle in the forward position as you approach a fence. If a rider sits back in his saddle with his reins quite long, when his horse takes off he must completely change his position to get forward and give his horse his head. **Never make sudden, quick motions as your horse approaches and takes off at a fence.**

A horse has a one-track mind. He can think of only one thing at a time. Certainly, when he jumps, his attention must be on the fence. If his rider has to make a big change in his position, this moving about will make the horse think about what the rider is doing, when he should have his mind on the approaching fence.

For this same reason, never suddenly throw your hands up on the back of your horse's neck, or give your horse a sharp kick, when you are just in front of a fence. If you distract your horse's attention by making quick, sudden moves, he will most certainly jump badly—if he jumps at all.

You may know your horse can jump a certain fence, but your horse may not know it; and he is the one who has to do the jumping. Encourage him, be ready to go with him and be sure to pat him when he has done well. Though he can't wag his tail like a dog, your horse really does like to be told when you are pleased.

Quiet stroking of your horse's neck and shoulder is a wonderful way to calm him when he is frightened or excited.

Enough of do's and don'ts. Try to remember them all, and work on your horsemanship—but most important of all, enjoy your jumping!

Riding Clothes

There are good reasons for the special cut and fit of riding clothes. Safety and comfort are the two biggest reasons, for well-fitting riding clothes give you a more secure grip in the saddle as well as the comfort that makes your riding a pleasure.

Riding clothes for young riders need not be expensive. The girl on the grey horse is wearing jodhpurs; they cover the whole leg and, if they fit snugly from the knee to the ankle, they are comfortable, easy to get on and off, as well as being attractive and suitable. Ankle-high boots, called jodhpur boots or shoes, are worn with "jodhs" and these are far less expensive than high boots.

The boy holding the horse is wearing boots and breeches. Breeches do not cover the whole leg; they button around the calf. If boots and breeches are worn the boots must fit perfectly, reaching well up to the knee and fitting snugly around the top of the leg. Because boots *must* fit so perfectly they are not always practical; young riders soon grow out of them.

Blue jeans or slacks of any kind are extremely uncomfortable, as they ride up and wrinkle around the rider's knees. If your legs are chafed you cannot ride well. It is just as easy to slip into a pair of jodhpurs.

Sneakers, or any shoes without heels, are dangerous. Boots have heels for a very good reason; they keep the stirrups where they belong. In a shoe without a heel your foot could slip all the way through the stirrup and, if you should happen to take a tumble, you would not be able to pull your foot out.

Wear cotton shirts when you ride, not blouses; shirts have tails that stay neatly tucked in.

EVEN FOR EVERYDAY RIDING, CLOTHES SHOULD BE NEAT, WELL-FITTING, AND COMFORTABLE

For more formal riding both these young riders have black coats, though coats of browns, greys, and tweeds also look well. Jodhpurs and breeches should be buff, brown or grey.

If you ride in a horse show, wear a tie; make sure your collar lies flat and unwrinkled and if the collar does not button down, wear a collar pin to keep it in place.

Both these riders are wearing hard black hunt caps.

Dress neatly when you ride. A well-cared-for horse always looks smart and trim, but if you are wearing sloppy clothes, you will make your horse look sloppy as well.

For formal riding of any kind, girls should either braid their hair or put it neatly into a net. Flowing locks are out of place on an otherwise smartly turned out rider.

If you wear neat, well-fitting riding clothes of quiet colors, no matter where you ride, you will always be suitably dressed.

Spurs should *not* be worn by inexperienced riders. If you don't have absolute control of your leg position, you are very apt to dig your horse with your spurs accidentally—and this usually happens at just the wrong moment.

Spurs are a delicate aid in schooling—not a means of punishment.

If you are a more advanced rider and feel you must wear spurs to help you in your schooling, be sure to wear them correctly.

They must be blunt; they must buckle toward the outside of your boot, with the buckle in the center; they must fit your boot tightly and be worn high on the heel, up by the seam. If this sounds too precise and confusing, don't worry about it—you're better off without them, anyway.

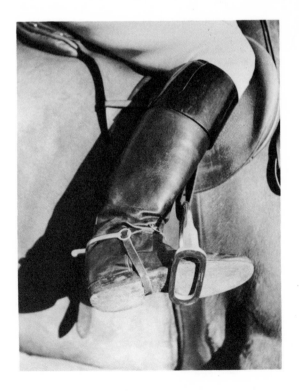

CORRECT ADJUSTMENT OF SPURS

A Horse of Your Own

Not everyone is lucky enough to have his own horse. Those of you who ride school horses should not be disappointed if they do not respond quickly to your signals.

These horses are ridden by all types of riders. Some of them are good, but others ride with their arms and legs everywhere, hanging onto the reins to keep their balance. The poor horse never knows whether a touch of a heel means canter, or just that his rider doesn't know what he is doing.

This doesn't mean, however, that you can't learn a great deal from these horses. Every time you put your foot in the stirrup you can learn something new—if you want to.

Whenever you ride, ride as well as you can. So often young riders are seen on slow, sleepy horses, kicking them carelessly and hauling on the reins. These riders think that since the horse doesn't seem to mind, they can ride as badly as they like. They are making a mistake, of course, because they will never get a chance to ride a really good horse until they can prove that they can ride *any* horse well. A highly-strung, well-schooled horse is a delight to ride, but he cannot stand indifferent horsemanship. Don't spoil the fun you could have, through your own carelessness.

Riding a school horse is never the same as having your own, of course, and if you don't have one now, perhaps you soon will. Those of you who are just beginning to ride, however, should not be in too much of a hurry. The more horses you can ride at the start, the faster you will learn. You don't want to find that you can ride your own horse well, but be completely lost when you ride a strange one—and this can happen too easily.

If the wonderful day comes when it is decided that you are to have a horse of your own, you should know how to find just the right horse.

First of all, you must decide what kind of a horse you want. There are horses for every purpose; beginners' horses, show horses, horses that jump and others that don't. *Take your time.* Consider each one carefully. Don't make the heart-breaking mistake of getting the very first horse that just might do. Make it a point to look at more than one; three or four would be even better, before you make up your mind.

WHAT TO LOOK FOR

No matter how good a rider you may be, no matter how much experience you have had, the very first thing to look for in your future horse is *manners.* "Manners" means a good mouth so your horse will turn and respond easily to the reins; a kind, sensible disposition; willingness to go on and do what he is told quickly, cheerfully, and in a friendly way.

Cross off your list any horse with a sour, mean disposition; any horse that is sulky or cross, that shows any signs of not wanting to leave his stable, or of wanting his own way. No matter how beautiful this horse may be; no matter how many other nice things there are about him, you can't have much fun riding a horse like this. In other words, don't buy other people's mistakes. It doesn't pay.

A horse with a nice head, big, dark eyes with an honest expression, that gives you the impression of intelligence and common sense, is practically sure to have a good disposition. If you will look

THIS 12.2 HAND PONY IS OF A
SUITABLE SIZE AND IS A GOOD
MOUNT FOR ITS YOUNG RIDER

back at the horses used to illustrate this book you will see that every one has a nice head and expression. They all have good width between their eyes, which is another sign of intelligence.

The horse's *conformation,* or build, is important. Although you must not expect perfect conformation unless you are prepared to pay well for it, you should look for the following good points:

A lean neck, slightly arched from the poll to just in front of the withers (a short or heavy-necked horse cannot "give" with any suppleness to the bit); a long, sloping line from the withers to the point of the shoulder, which gives the horse the ability to move with an easy, low stride, close to the ground; a broad chest, short back, strong hindquarters and ribs well arched, for strength and endurance; hocks, knees, and fetlocks sturdy, but not coarse; tendons straight and clean-cut.

All together, look for a horse or pony which stands and moves squarely with a natural balance, giving an over-all picture of strength without coarseness and fineness of line without weakness.

A lot depends on what you want your horse to be able to do. If you have not had much riding experience, look for a horse that is quiet and sensible, but not dull and sleepy. Don't make the mistake of thinking that just any old horse will do to get you started. A willing, obedient horse can start you out on years of riding pleasure, just as a sour, clumsy animal can spoil your fun so completely that you might never want to ride again.

Suitability is important. A suitable horse is one the right size for you. Large ponies or small horses are excellent for small riders.

Horses and ponies are measured in hands; a hand is four inches.

To measure a horse for height, be sure, first of all, to stand him squarely on all four legs on level ground; a cement surface is perfect. Measure from the ground to the top of his shoulders, or withers, and divide the number of inches by four.

If he is sixty-three inches, he is fifteen hands, three inches high, or "fifteen-three."

Fourteen and a half hands, or 14.2, is the height division between horses and ponies. A pony is always 14.2 or under; a horse is always over 14.2 hands.

Ponies and horses ranging in height from fourteen to fifteen, or fifteen and a half hands, are a suitable size for children. For taller riders you can go up to horses 16.2; horses any bigger than this are really too big.

There are some ponies from 12.2 hands up to 13.3 that do make good mounts for young riders. If you are considering a pony in this height range, make absolutely sure that he has a kind disposition and excellent manners.

Smaller ponies, under 12.2, are extremely clever and appealing. Many of these small ponies, however, are apt to be a little too independent to be much fun to ride. Some of them are quite bad-tempered. It sometimes takes a while for this to show, so if you are considering a small pony, do be very careful to make sure he has nice manners before you make up your mind.

For an inexperienced rider a horse should not be under seven and not over fourteen years old. Young horses are apt to be too gay and though an old horse is usually quiet and sensible, if he is too old you take the chance of losing him, which is always a hard blow.

Don't make the mistake of getting a really outstanding horse if you are an inexperienced rider. A well-bred, good-looking horse is very nice to own, but is bound to be pretty much of a handful. It is far better to get a quiet horse with perfect manners, with the understanding that when you have learned all you can from him, you will sell him and get another.

THIS HALF-THOROUGHBRED HORSE
IS AN EXCELLENT TYPE; A GOOD
MOUNT FOR A YOUNG RIDER

For the more experienced rider, a lot still depends on what you want to do with your horse. Be sure the horse you are considering has good manners, first of all, and the ability to do what you want. If you want to jump, be sure the horse can jump well. If you plan to hunt some day, or ride in horse shows eventually, keep this in mind.

If you are planning to go on into hunting or showing, it would be a good idea to get a horse with some quality, or Thoroughbred blood. Thoroughbred blood gives a horse a sleeker coat, a finer, better-looking head, smoother lines, and the ability to move easily and to jump well. A half-Thoroughbred, or half-bred horse, makes a wonderful horse for a young rider, combining the sparkle and smooth, easy way of going of the Thoroughbred with the quieter disposition of other breeds.

Don't think just because a horse has Thoroughbred blood that he has to be terribly expensive. This isn't true. And, what's more, don't forget—it costs just as much to keep a stodgy, cold-blooded animal as it does to keep a good horse, with not nearly as much pleasure as the good horse will give you.

Whatever you do, don't buy a weedy, ugly horse just because he is inexpensive. If you take your time you will find a nice horse for the price you want to pay. A cheap horse may be a bargain when you buy him, but though your horse doesn't have to be a world-beater, you should, at least, be proud and happy to own him.

WHERE TO LOOK

Once you have decided on the kind of horse you want and the price you want to pay, the next step is to find him.

Go to the horse dealers around your part of the country; keep your eyes and ears open and let people know you are looking for a horse. If there are horse shows nearby, go to see them. If you see a horse there you like, speak to his owner; he certainly won't mind, as it is a compliment that you like his horse so much, and it just might be for sale.

TRYING OUT A HORSE YOU LIKE

When you have found a horse that seems to be what you want at the price you want to pay, arrange to try him out.

Watch the horse when he is being saddled and bridled; you don't want a horse that kicks or bites when he is being handled.

Whether or not you are experienced, take a friend with you who can ride and ask him to try the horse first. Watch the horse walk, trot and canter and, if you are interested in jumping, see that the horse is taken over a few fences.

Don't pay any attention to a horse that is jumped without a rider, either being chased over a jump or led over it on a long rope. Some horses are spectacular jumpers when they are loose, but can hardly get over a three-foot fence with a rider. If the horse can't be jumped right then, with someone on his back, forget him.

If you still like the horse, get on him yourself. Don't let anyone hold him while you mount and arrange your reins and stirrups.

Walk, trot, and canter him, and pop him over a fence or two. Remember, though, not to wear the poor horse out. He is for sale and there may be others planning to try him the same day. Ride him enough to get a good idea of what he is like, but if you aren't seriously interested, have the consideration to get off.

If you don't like the horse, thank the owner and go away. If you do like him, arrange for a more thorough try-out. Ride him away from the stable, with other horses and alone. Test him, within reason, in every way you can, always keeping this in mind: **Can he do the job you want him to do? Has he the ability to do it well?**

Remember that he is to be *your* horse. No matter what anyone else may say, no matter how wonderful the horse is said to be, if you don't like him, forget him. After all, *you* are the one who is going to work with him, ride him, and love him—and you are the one who must be pleased.

When you have tried at least two horses—three or four would be better still—and have chosen the one you like best, *now* is the time to say to the owner: "I like your horse and I will take him if he is passed by my veterinarian as sound."

Any intelligent owner of a horse, whether he is a friend or a stranger, knows you and your family are making an investment, and you have to be sure you are getting what you want. Even if the horse is offered to you as a gift, or by a friend, be polite but firm about having the horse passed by the veterinarian of *your* choice. If the owner becomes angry, or hurt, you have saved yourself a veterinary fee; there is something the matter with the horse.

Don't believe that asking a vet to pass on a horse is admitting and advertising your ignorance. It doesn't matter whether or not you know the difference between a spavin and a thoroughpin; no matter how much or how little you or a friend may know, you don't have the experience, the qualifications or the training of a veterinarian who has years of study of horses behind him.

He will tactfully go over the horse looking for signs of weakness in heart and wind; he will check the horse's eyesight and the condition of his legs and feet.

A *sound* horse is one that has perfect sight in both eyes; his heart and lungs are normal, and his legs and hoofs are strong and without any blemish that might one day cause lameness. A horse that is unsound in any way should be turned down at once.

If the veterinarian tells you that to the best of his knowledge, the horse is sound, you will take the horse with the comfortable assurance that you are starting out well. The veterinarian's small fee might very well save you from a sad experience; suppose the horse you planned to take had, for instance, a bad heart!

One more thing to remember: Don't buy a very thin horse. Such a horse can be as sound as a bell, but nine times out of ten his trouble is between the ears. A horse that rears, for example, can be literally starved out of his bad tricks until he is quiet enough to be sold. After a little care and good feed, the old tricks come back in full force and you are left with a worthless horse on your hands.

The one horse out of ten that is nothing more than badly cared for—and you can't tell the difference until it is too late—will be a completely different animal after a few good meals. More often than not he turns out to be far too much horse for his new owner. So **don't buy any horse in very poor condition.**

If you have taken your time and used careful common sense, you are now—or soon will be—the proud owner of a new horse. A horse with manners, and gaits that you like; a horse that can do the job you want him to do with the ability to do it well; a horse that has been passed by your veterinarian as sound. You've not bought a "bargain"; you're off to a good start.

If you find that you have made a mistake in buying a horse, if you find after a time that he is not suitable, have the intelligence and common sense to get rid of him. There isn't a horseman anywhere that hasn't made the same mistake at some time; you're not the first to have this happen. The horseman admits he was wrong and either sells or gives the horse away as soon as he possibly can. It is the only thing to do. There are lots of other horses in the world that *can* do and *will* do what you ask of them; why should you be satisfied with anything else?

A CAREFULLY CHOSEN HORSE WILL BRING MANY HOURS OF COMPANIONSHIP AND PLEASURE

Riding in Horse Shows

Horse shows are growing more and more popular throughout the country, as the one-horse owners discover the fun and success they can have in the show ring. Showing is no longer limited to the expensive show stables with a number of top horses; the owner and exhibitor of one horse has every chance of doing as well in horse show competition.

Another reason for the growing popularity of shows is the larger number of children's classes that are being offered. In these classes young riders can compete against others of their own age and ability. Shows that offer a number of these classes will get a larger entry, for although no one can win a ribbon in every class at every show, each young rider quite naturally wants to know that he has at least a fair chance of doing well.

Choose a local, one-day event for your first show. The competition won't be as difficult, the fences won't be as high, and it won't seem as confusing as a bigger show.

If you are not on the show's mailing list—and you probably won't be if this is your first experience—posters will tell you how to get information, including the prize list.

The *prize list* of a horse show lists all the classes the show is offering, with the description of the classes and of the trophies and ribbons to be awarded.

In *horsemanship* classes you will be judged on your seat and hands, management and control of your horse. There are a number of ways horsemanship classes can be divided.

A *maiden* horsemanship class is for children who have never won a blue ribbon in a horsemanship class;

THE WINNER OF A HORSEMANSHIP CLASS RECEIVING HER RIBBON FROM THE RINGMASTER

WAITING AT RING GATE FOR
THEIR CLASS TO BE CALLED

A *novice* is one who has not won three blue ribbons;

A *limit* is one who has never won six blue ribbons.

The *open* horsemanship class is open to all young riders, no matter how many ribbons they have won.

All horsemanship classes can be divided into different age groups, such as: "Open Horsemanship, hunter seat; for those under 13 years of age."

Horsemanship classes can be held over jumps, or on the "flat"; walk, trot, canter and hand-gallop without any jumping; or on the flat first, with six or eight riders chosen by the judges to jump. The prize list will give you this information.

For instance, you may find a class like this: "Horsemanship, hunter seat. Over 3′ fences. Open to all children fifteen years of age and under. Trophy and six ribbons."

This class will be held in the ring; each rider enters the ring alone and jumps six or eight fences, three feet high; the rider whom the judges consider the best will receive a trophy and the blue ribbon; the next five best riders will each receive a ribbon.

RIDING IN HORSEMANSHIP CLASSES

In horsemanship classes on the flat, all the contestants enter the ring together. You will be asked to ride at a walk, trot and canter; you may be asked to hand-gallop.

Keep your mind on what you are doing. Ride as well as you possibly can. Every aspect of your horsemanship will be judged; not only how you look, but how you turn your horse and how you control him.

At the walk, have your horse walking briskly, while you keep a soft contact with his mouth. An alert, balanced horse is a sign of good horsemanship.

Remember your diagonals when the ringmaster calls for the class to trot. Try not to look down at your horse's shoulder. Don't forget to sit to the first few strides. Have your horse moving at a smart trot, but keep him steady and balanced. Don't work at your posting; keep as close to the saddle as you can. Keep your hands still, your head up; look where you are going.

When you are asked to canter, it will probably be from a walk. Take your time. Shorten your reins quietly, steady and collect your horse, then break him off on the correct lead. You certainly should be able to tell which lead you are on without looking.

Canter smoothly and easily—and slowly.

When you are told to walk again, pull up quietly, hands down.

When you are asked to reverse, turn your horse toward the ring fence. Don't forget to use your legs properly.

If you are asked to gallop, let your horse move right along

down the length of the ring, then sit up a little and steady him smoothly around the turns.

In all ring riding, look out for the other horses. Don't cut too close in front of another horse. If you find yourself crowded in a bunch, make a circle at one end of the ring to get to a clear space where you can be seen. After all, how can you be judged if you huddle by the rail with four or five horses between you and the center of the ring!

Don't keep looking at the judges! Your horse may barge right into the quarters of the horse ahead of him, or break stride; keep your eyes and mind on what you are doing.

In jumping classes, each contestant enters the ring by himself. When it is your turn, be ready. If your horse is standing half-asleep, give him a sharp kick to wake him up as the gate opens to get him on his toes. Have your reins short enough so you won't have to fuss with them in the ring.

Ride through the gate and make a wide circle to the right at a walk or trot. As your circle brings you near the ring fence, break your horse smoothly into a canter—on the correct lead.

Look up at the first fence and keep your eyes on this fence as you turn and canter toward it. As soon as your horse is moving in a straight line toward the fence, let him go on a little faster, giving him a strong squeeze with your legs if necessary.

After he has landed, touch him lightly on the mouth to steady

LINED UP IN THE CENTER OF THE RING
AS THE JUDGES MAKE THEIR DECISION

ARTIFICIAL STONE WALL IN
A CHILDREN'S JUMPER CLASS

and balance him without slowing him down, keeping your eyes on the second fence as you ride toward it in a straight line.

After the second fence, keep up out of the saddle but straighten a little as you steady your horse around the turn. As he approaches the third fence, let him move on again.

You will probably be told to go twice around the ring over the fences. Do not at any time let your horse break into a trot around the turns or between jumps.

After the last fence sit down in your saddle, pull up, and leave the ring at a walk.

In horsemanship classes, it does not count against you if your horse knocks down a rail.

If your horse refuses a fence, don't get flustered. Let him stand for a moment at the fence he refused, then turn him and ride him at it again, using your legs more strongly.

Three refusals usually mean that you are eliminated. After the third refusal, have the good sportsmanship to turn and ride quietly out of the ring.

In horse show language your turn in the ring over fences, or over an outside course, is called a "round." After your round, stay near the ring, pat your horse, and let him relax. The judges might want to call you back into the ring with four or five others, so don't wander off too far.

If you are called into the ring, the judges may ask you and the others to ride, for example, in a figure eight. Listen to their instructions carefully and don't hesitate to ask questions if you don't understand.

CLASSES FOR YOUR HORSE

Besides horsemanship classes, in which the rider is judged, many shows have classes in which the horse is judged. These classes include:

Children's Hacks. Sometimes the prize list will specify hunter type, or saddle type, or both. If you ever have anything to do with the organization of a horse show, don't let the committee combine hunter and saddle types in any class, including horsemanship. Combining them isn't fair to the horses, their owners, or the judges.

In a hack class, your horse will be judged at a walk, trot, and canter, both ways of the ring. He will be judged on his manners and mouth, way of going, and suitability.

Make sure you respond to the different requests promptly to show your horse is quick to do as you ask. Ride at a brisk walk, a free and balanced trot, and a slow, collected canter.

Even though your horsemanship is not being judged, don't ride sloppily! A careful rider on a good horse will always make a better impression than an equally good horse ridden carelessly.

Children's Hunter Hacks. You will ride first as you would in an ordinary hack class, then the judges will select six or eight of the horses they like the best to jump two or four fences in the ring. If you are asked to jump, let your horse move on at a hand-gallop toward the fences, a little faster than in the horsemanship

TAKING AN AIKEN FENCE IN
A CHILDREN'S HUNTER CLASS

A GOOD RIDER ON A BOLD JUMPER TAKING A GATE FENCE ON THE OUTSIDE COURSE AT A SHOW

classes. The judges want to see your horse jump freely, right out of his stride, while still under perfect control.

Children's Hunters. This class can be held either in the ring or over an outside course. An outside course, as the name suggests, is set up outside the ring where there can be longer distances between the fences and where the fences themselves can be more solidly built and of different types.

The horses in this class go one at a time, whether in the ring or over a course, and are judged on mouth, manners, way of going (way of moving; a good hunter moves smoothly and effortlessly), style of jumping, and suitability as a child's hunter.

When your number is called to jump, start out smoothly with your reins short enough for full control, and have your horse moving at a steady hand-gallop so he is balanced and striding evenly by the time you reach the first fence.

Don't let your horse gallop too fast; a children's hunter should not show too much speed, but should give the impression of excellent manners and safety.

If a fence on the course has more than one section, or *panel*, make up your mind, well before you reach it, which panel you plan

A YOUNG RIDER SHOWING GOOD FORM JUMPING A BRUSH FENCE IN A HORSEMANSHIP CLASS

to jump, and stick to your choice. Nothing confuses a horse more than a rider who either can't make up his mind which panel to take, or who changes his mind at the last minute.

If there is an in-and-out on the course—an in-and-out consists of two fences, set from twenty-four to thirty feet apart—make sure your horse jumps the same panel in *and* out. If he jumps, for instance, the left panel going in, then takes a stride and jumps the right panel going out, he is said to have "cross-paneled," and this will count very much against him. After all, he is in a hunter class, and if there had been someone else jumping at your right, your horse would have swerved straight into him!

After all the horses in the class have had their rounds, the judges will call back six or eight of the best to be "jogged." This means the rider will be asked to trot his horse past the judges so they can be sure the horse is not lame; a lame horse cannot be awarded a ribbon in a hunter or in a hack class.

If this has been a *working* hunter class, the ribbons will then be awarded. In a *conformation* hunter class the horse's conformation, or build, will count, and the six or eight best horses will be lined up with their saddles off for conformation judging.

YOU SHOULD SEE THAT YOUR
HORSE STANDS WELL WHILE
CONFORMATION IS JUDGED

Make your horse stand squarely on all four legs while he is being judged. Keep his head up, and try to keep his ears pricked forward by attracting his attention.

The class specifications will tell how much conformation will count, if it counts at all. For example: "Children's Hunters. To be shown over the outside course, no fence to exceed three feet. Performance, manners, way of going, style of jumping, and suitability as a child's mount to count 75%; conformation 25%."

Children's Jumpers. "Jumper" classes are held in the ring and scored only on the faults your horse makes at each fence. Touching a fence with a fore or hind hoof, refusing or knocking down a rail are scored against him. The horse with the least number of faults wins the class. If two or more horses jump the course without any faults they are said to have gone "clean" and these horses will jump again with the fences raised three to six inches. If two or more horses are tied with the same number of faults, they jump again, until one horse scores a lower number of faults.

The class specifications will say, for example: "Children's Jumpers. Performance only to count. Fences starting at three feet; to be raised in the case of a tie. Trophy and four ribbons."

RIBBON AWARDS

After your class has been judged, the winner will receive

the blue ribbon and, usually, a trophy as well.

The red ribbon is for second place.

Yellow for third.

White for fourth.

If more than four ribbons are awarded, fifth place ribbon is pink; and sixth is green.

CHAMPIONSHIP AWARDS

Some shows offer a championship in the horsemanship division, and the first and second place winners in all horsemanship classes ride together in a special class. The winner receives the horsemanship championship ribbon; second place winner receives the reserve championship. Only two ribbons are awarded.

Championships in the children's horse division are usually awarded on a point basis; blue ribbons count five points; red, three; yellow, two; and white, one. Fifth and sixth ribbons do not count.

The horse winning the most points receives the championship ribbon, and is champion children's horse of the show; the horse with the second highest number of points is reserve champion.

The championship ribbon usually has three very long streamers; one blue, one red, and one yellow. The reserve championship is red, yellow and white.

COMPETING IN "MACLAY" HORSEMANSHIP CLASS AT THE NATIONAL HORSE SHOW, NEW YORK

Preparing Your Horse for a Show

A little extra effort a few days before a show can make all the difference in the looks of your horse.

With an electric clipping machine, or a pair of scissors, trim the shaggy hair from your horse's fetlocks so they will be smooth and neat. You will be pleased to see how this fines down the line of his legs.

Trim the long whiskers from his muzzle.

If your horse has white markings, wash them in warm water with a little ordinary blueing; then dry them carefully.

If your horse's tail is grey or white, you can wash it with warm water and a mild soap (*not* laundry soap); rinse it thoroughly with warm water, and let it dry. When it has dried completely, brush it out gently.

The day of the show, after he has been groomed, take a soft cloth and go over his coat the way the hair lies; this will add a little extra polish that will make him shine.

Braiding a horse's mane shows off the line of his head and neck. It is not a difficult thing to do, and it does look very nice.

To braid a mane: Starting behind your horse's ears, take a section of mane about the width of four fingers, dividing it neatly from the rest of the mane with a comb. Dampen this lock of mane with a brush dipped in water and braid it tightly. When you have braided it down to the end, turn the braid under and fasten it right up against your horse's neck with a small, plain-colored rubber band.

Do the entire mane this way, finishing up by making one neat braid of the forelock. You will be delighted at how smart and trim this makes your horse look.

Braid his mane either the night before, or the morning of the show; if it is left up too long, your horse will start rubbing it be-

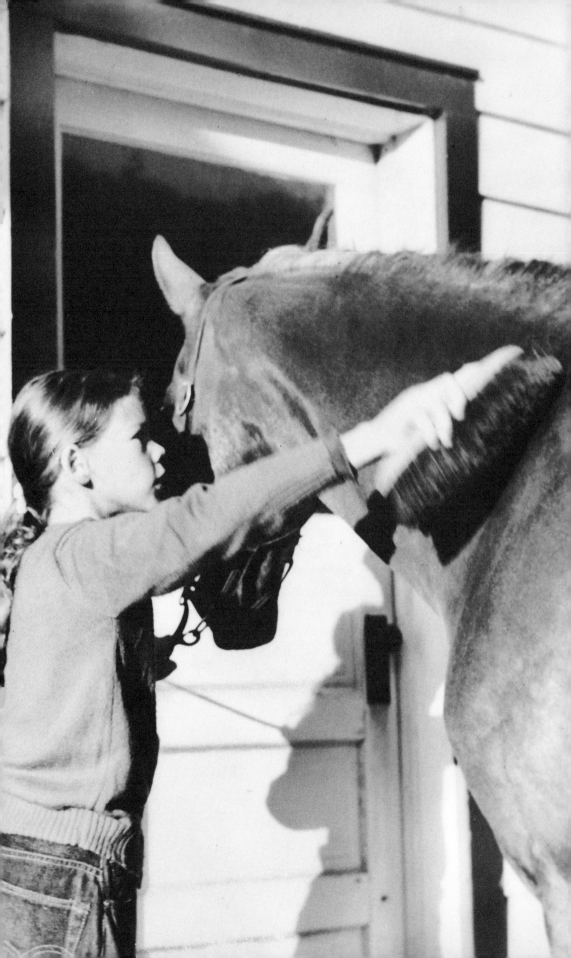

cause it has become uncomfortable. This breaks off some of the hairs and when you finally do let the mane down, it will look ragged.

Hunters often have their tails braided when they are shown, but this is not as easy as braiding a mane. If your horse's tail is well brushed-out and the top hair is smoothed down with a damp brush, it will look very nice and need not be braided.

Your bridle and saddle should be well saddle-soaped and your stirrup irons, buckles, and bit should be polished until they sparkle. Don't feel you must have brand new tack just because you are going in a show. Older, well-cared-for tack looks far nicer. If you do happen to have a new bridle or new reins, however, be sure they are soaped and stained until they are quite dark. The bright yellow of new tack does not look well.

On the day of the show, plan to arrive at the grounds in plenty of time so you won't feel rushed. If this is your first show, ride your horse quietly around the grounds so he can get used to the loud-speaker and the crowds.

Check your tack over carefully before you get up; it would be very sad to have lost a class just because your horse was fussing from a carelessly twisted curb chain! Especially before each jumping class, warm your horse up by a few minutes of walking, trotting and cantering. This will loosen up his muscles and get you settled in the saddle.

Check the girth once more before going into the ring.

After each class, if your horse is hot, dismount, loosen his girth a couple of holes and walk him slowly until he is quite dry. Whatever you do, don't sit on his back or ride him around all day long. Give him every chance you can to relax. In horsemanship classes, as well as classes for the horse himself, he will make a far better showing if he is rested and fresh.

Most important of all, have a good time! Blue ribbons and silver trophies are very nice, but only one person in each class can win them! Enjoy yourself, ride as well as you can—and good luck!

Glossary

Balance: A horse is balanced when his weight is on all four legs, with hind legs drawn far enough under body to be easily used in starting, stopping, turning, and moving forward at all gaits.

Break off on a lead: To start cantering on a specified lead; "to break off on the left lead" is to start cantering on the left lead.

Cold-blooded horse: A horse that is not pure Thoroughbred.

Common: An expression describing a coarse, clumsy horse.

Contact: A light, constant feel on the bit through the rider's hands and reins.

Diagonal: At the trot, the horse's left foreleg and right hind leg move forward together in one stride; this is the left diagonal. Then the right foreleg and left hind leg move in the next stride; this is the right diagonal. As the rider posts to the trot, rising as the left foreleg moves forward and sinking into the saddle as this leg moves back, he is posting on the left diagonal. If he rises as the right foreleg moves forward and sinks as it comes back, he is posting on the right diagonal. The correct diagonal when trotting in a circle is that on the outside of the circle. (Circling to the right, rider should be on left diagonal.)

Figure eight: A schooling exercise. (See pages 54 and 60.)

Float: To rasp a horse's teeth, smoothing off the rough edges that develop after a period of time. This should be done by a veterinarian once a year.

Forehand: The part of the horse in front of the saddle; head, neck, shoulders, and forelegs.

Forging: The horse striking the toe of the forehoof with the toe of the hind shoe, making a clicking sound with each stride at the trot.

Forward seat: A balanced seat which allows full freedom to the horse's natural motions and balance while the rider is in the position to aid, guide, and control him.

Gaits: The horse's natural gaits are the walk, trot and gallop; the canter is a slow, collected gallop.

Getting under a fence: The horse coming so close to a fence before taking off that he jumps awkwardly; putting in an extra short stride before taking off.

Hack: A horse kept primarily for pleasure riding without being asked to do much jumping.
A word sometimes used to describe a riding-school horse.

To hack: To ride a horse at a walk, trot and canter; to ride quietly from one place to another, as "to hack from the stable to the horse show."

Hack Classes: Bridle Path Hacks: A class in a horse show in which the horses are judged at a walk, trot and canter as a well-mannered, comfortable ride.
Hunter Hacks: A horse show class in which the horses are first judged at a walk, trot, canter, and hand-gallop; six or eight are then chosen by the judges to jump two or four fences, usually in the ring, to show manners and jumping ability.

Hand: A unit used in measuring the height of horses and ponies; a hand is four inches.

Half-bred: A half-Thoroughbred horse; a horse with one Thoroughbred parent and the other of unknown or of other than pure Thoroughbred breeding.

Head-shy: Term used to describe a horse afraid to have his head touched, who throws his head up in fright at the gesture of a hand. A sign of ill-treatment.

Hindquarters: The part of the horse behind the saddle; quarters and hind legs.

Hunter: A horse kept primarily for following hounds.

Hunter class: A horse show class in which the horses are judged on their manners, performance, way of going, style of jumping and soundness over an outside course or over fences in the ring.

Working hunters are judged only on their performance and soundness; **Conformation hunters** are judged on performance, soundness, and conformation; the percentage specified in the prize list.

Hunter Type: A horse of such conformation as to make him suitable for hunting, even though he may be used only as a hack or show horse. For description of hunter-type conformation, see page 93.

Hunting distance: Seven or eight horses' lengths between riders; a safe distance giving a rider time enough to pull up should the horse in front of him fall or lose his rider.

Jog: To lead or ride a horse at a slow trot, as to jog a horse before the judges, enabling them to see whether or not the horse is lame; a lame horse cannot be awarded a ribbon in a hack or hunter class at a horse show.

Keeper: Small leather loop near buckles to keep loose ends of straps in place.

Lead: At the canter or gallop, the horse leads with one foreleg that reaches further out with each stride than the other. When the left foreleg reaches further than the right, the horse is on the left lead. The lead supports the horse's weight as he turns at the canter or gallop.

Manners: The horse's behavior. A horse with good manners is obedient, sensible; does not kick or bite; responds quickly and easily to the bit, and does not take advantage of his rider in any way.

Near side: The left side of a horse.

Off side: The right side of a horse.

Post: To rise and sink in the saddle in rhythm with the horse's trotting stride.

Prize list: The list sent out before a horse show, describing the classes to be held, ribbons, trophies and other awards to be given, the show rules, and names of the judges.

Refusal: The horse stopping at a fence, refusing to jump.

Run-out: A form of refusal when, instead of stopping, the horse swerves away from the fence or runs around it.

Saddle Horse: A breed of horse whose full name is American Saddle Horse. Instead of the long, low gaits of the hunter, the Saddle Horse lifts his hoofs high, bending his knees and hocks extensively with precision and spirit; his head and tail are carried high, giving an over-all picture of brilliance, grace, and proud bearing.

Saddle seat: The horsemanship used in riding Saddle Horses, adapted to "lift" their high action and exhibit their brilliant way of going.

School: To train a horse.

Stopper: Small rubber loop used to keep running or standing martingale strap from sliding through the neck strap.

Also, a small leather piece slid onto reins between the bit and running martingale rings to prevent the rings from catching in the rein buckle at the bit.

Sound: Term used to describe a horse who has perfect sight in both eyes; whose heart and wind are normal; who is not lame and whose legs and hoofs are free from any blemish that might cause lameness.

Tack: The equipment used on the horse, such as the saddle, bridle, and martingale.

To tack up: To put the saddle and bridle on the horse, or other such equipment used on the horse.

Timing: Judging the approach to a fence; knowing exactly where and when the horse will take off at a fence.

Way of going: The horse's way of moving.

Weedy: Term used to describe a horse without substance or depth; light in the body; giving the appearance of weakness in build.

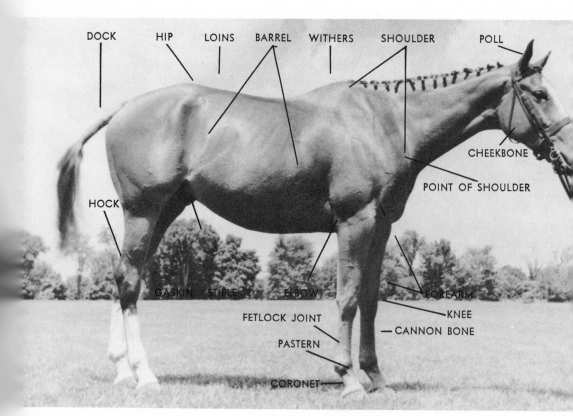

POINTS OF THE HORSE

Index

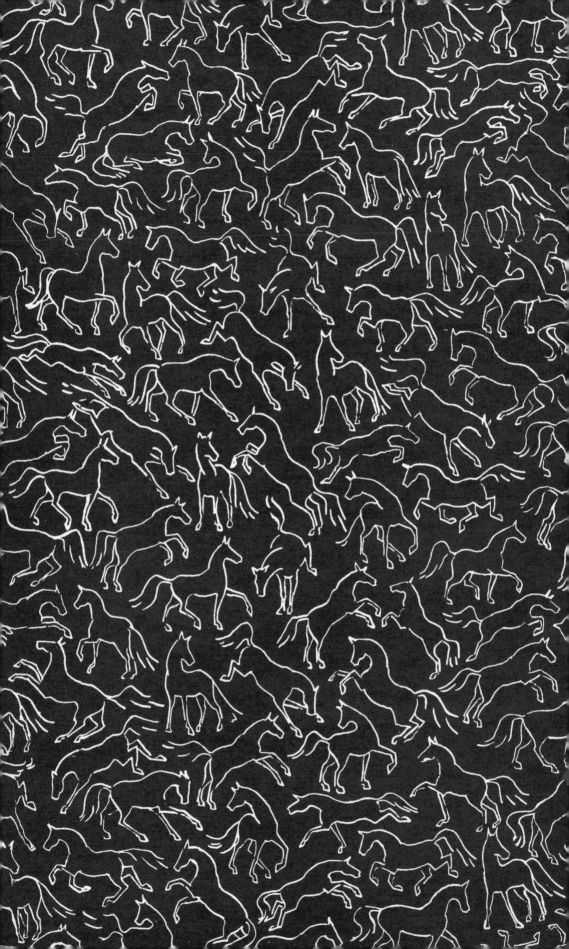